TRANSFORMING
SYSTEMS

Praise for the book

This book is a treasure. In this rapidly changing, deeply disorienting digital age, it helps us reset our ethical compass and thereby reconnect us to our essential humanity. It does so independently of your national, cultural, ethnic and religious allegiances. Extraordinary.

—Dennis Snower, President,
Global Solutions Initiative

Humanity is facing multiple existential challenges. We have to learn how to reshape the underlying systems with new mindsets and tools, and deeply ethical leadership from many more of us. This is the powerful message of Arun's new book which covers an enormous intellectual terrain in a very engaging way.

—Ravi Venkatesan, Business leader, Philanthropist and UNICEF'S Special Representative for Young People and Innovation

Arun Maira speaks and writes only when he has something distinctive to say—and that is what he does in this book, once again. I feel certain that the reader will think deeply about a business world in which ethical assets matter a lot more than today. A great read.

—R. Gopalakrishnan, Former Executive Director, Tata Sons, and Former Vice-Chairman, Hindustan Unilever

Arun Maira has explained in a compelling way why business corporations cannot survive in a society that fails. He offers a new ethical toolkit for both corporations and young leaders based on less self-absorption, more care for the less fortunate, and greater concern for our Mother Earth.

—Anu Aga, Corporate Social Action Leader

Transforming Systems is one of the most thought-provoking books I have read in years. Arun Maira, who skilfully using the story telling technique, will make you pause ever so often, reflect, analyse, relearn, and almost co-create the new toolkit with him. A profound yet easy-to-read contribution to the literature on solving social inequality.

—Ajit Rangnekar, Former Dean,
Indian School of Business

TRANSFORMING SYSTEMS

Why the World Needs a
NEW ETHICAL TOOLKIT

ARUN MAIRA

RUPA

Published by
Rupa Publications India Pvt. Ltd 2019
7/16, Ansari Road, Daryaganj
New Delhi 110002

Sales centres:
Allahabad Bengaluru Chennai
Hyderabad Jaipur Kathmandu
Kolkata Mumbai

Copyright © Arun Maira 2019

The views and opinions expressed in this book are the author's own and the facts are as reported by her which have been verified to the extent possible, and the publishers are not in any way liable for the same.

All rights reserved.
No part of this publication may be reproduced, transmitted,
or stored in a retrieval system, in any form or by any means,
electronic, mechanical, photocopying, recording or otherwise,
without the prior permission of the publisher.

ISBN: 978-93-5333-574-8

First impression 2019

10 9 8 7 6 5 4 3 2 1

The moral right of the author has been asserted.

Printed by Replika Press Pvt. Ltd., India

This book is sold subject to the condition that it shall not, by way
of trade or otherwise, be lent, resold, hired out, or otherwise circulated,
without the publisher's prior consent, in any form of binding
or cover other than that in which it is published.

Contents

Foreword   vii

Introduction   xi

PART A
Aspirations to Improve the World

1. The Purpose of Our Lives   2
2. Redesigning an Airplane While Flying   6
3. What You Care About Deeply   14
4. Searching for a Better Way   19
5. How Will AI Machines Learn Ethics?   29
6. Partnerships for the SDGs   39
7. The Origins of Ethical Foundations   48
8. Shutting Out 'People Not Like Us'   57

PART B
Search for a New Paradigm

9. Learning to Listen   70
10. Shapes and Sizes of Systems   74
11. Local Solutions to Global Problems   83
12. Unlearning and Rethinking   91
13. Three Models of Systems   97
14. Systems' Structures   113

PART C
Reorienting Our Minds

15.	Taking Charge of Our Own Stories	128
16.	Two Paradigms for Managing Change	138
17.	Systems Thinking	146
18.	Ethics of Citizenship	158
19.	Deep Listening	169
20.	Networked Organizations	176
21.	Learning to Learn	186

PART D
Becoming a Leader

22.	Learning to Lead	202

Index   215

Foreword

Adam Kahane

In this book, Arun Maira and the people he writes about explore how to live a good life and how to make a difference in the world. Can I attend to my needs and also to those of my community? Is it better to work for a company or an NGO? How do I stand up for what I think is right and yet leave space for others? Gradually, Arun shows us that there are no single right answers to these questions. Even though we might yearn for a simple straight path, there isn't one. We can only feel our way forward, in our own particular context, learning as we go—as Arun has done in his own life. The Spanish poet Antonio Machado wrote about this approach: 'Walker, there is no path. The path is made by walking.'

Arun's message is vital because these days, around the world, the thirst for one right answer—in professional life, in morality, in politics—is increasingly strong and dangerous. He points us to another, more peaceful, less travelled way.

When I was at university in Montreal and Berkeley, I studied theoretical physics and mathematical economics. I was clever and confident and it seemed obvious to me that every problem had one correct solution that smart people could figure out and implement. After I graduated I took a job in the global strategic planning department of Royal Dutch Shell, the energy company, in 1988 in London. This was a time and place besotted with one triumphalist right answer—capitalism and competition and companies were the best way to address all societal challenges everywhere. The Thatcherite political slogan that summarized this answer was

TINA—There Is No Alternative.

In 1991, Shell seconded me to support a team of 28 leaders in South Africa who wanted to use the company's scenario-planning methodology to help effect a transformation from apartheid to democracy. This team was made up of people from across all sectors of South African society—black and white, establishment and opposition, right and left; from politics, business, academia, trade unions, and civil society. They most definitely didn't agree on any single answer; they didn't agree on what the solution was, or even on what the problem was; they knew that there were multiple alternatives. This was the first time I had participated in such a dialogic process, and I was amazed by how creatively and productively this diverse group was able to work together to move their country forward. This experience radically changed my understanding of what I needed to do with my life, and I ended up leaving Shell and taking up a vocation as a facilitator of such multi-stakeholder processes to address complex societal challenges.

In 2006, I worked in India on a large project to reduce the rate of child malnutrition in the state of Maharashtra. It involved 26 organizations, including international and state agencies, local NGOs, and multi-national companies such as Unilever and Tata. By then, I had met Arun and he gave me a lot of help in navigating this ambitious and challenging undertaking. This type of collaboration was unfamiliar in India and the dynamics in the team were often tangled and tense. At one point I found myself overwhelmed and confused, and I went to Arun and asked him what it was that we were really doing. His answer was insightful and guides me still: 'You have to member, Adam, that typically in such a multi-actor undertaking, 100 per cent of the actors arrive thinking that if only the *others* would change what they are doing, the problem would be solved. But if all of the parties are in the room, then it can't be all someone else's fault! What we are really doing is enabling these actors to see that they might have to change what they themselves are doing.'

The main thing that I have learned over these years, then, is that, contrary to what I thought when I started out; we always have to work out, in our particular context and moment, what we ourselves need to do to make our way forward. This means that we need to be aware of the larger system of which we are part, and at the same time to focus on our own role and responsibility, and ultimately, only, on our own next step. This pragmatic, tentative, humble orientation is crucial in a world increasingly saturated by harsh certainties about what others must do, and the polarisation and violence that these create. If you want to live a good life and to make a difference in the world, peacefully, then you need to learn to work patiently with the multiplicity and conflict both around you and inside you. For this journey Arun has written an excellent guidebook.

Adam Kahane is a director of Reos Partners and the author of *Solving Tough Problems*, *Power and Love*, *Transformative Scenario Planning*, and *Collaborating with the Enemy*.

Introduction

> Forgive, O Lord, my little jokes on Thee
> And I'll forgive Thy great big one on me.
>
> (Robert Frost, *The Poetry of Robert Frost*,
> Jonathan Cape, 1971)

'Are we real, or are we a story?' my seven-year old granddaughter asked her mother one day. My daughter passed on the question up another generation—to me. Having lived longer, I should have thought about it before.

'Who am I?' and 'What is my role in the world which I am a part of?' are existential questions that often arise in human minds. Human beings live, along with other humans and species, within a complex world composed of many natural and social systems. While other animals seem satisfied to 'live and die and never question why', such profound questions arise only in human minds.

Robert Frost suggests that the capacity to question the purpose of one's own existence, for which there is no easy answer, is the big joke that god has played on humans. Human beings sense that they are part of a larger story. They wonder what this story is. Human beings have aspirations—that as far as we know, no other species has—to change the big story of which they are a small part.

People want to tame animals and harness nature to meet their requirements. New technologies, developed with human intelligence, have enabled humans to increase their power on nature enormously. Humans have been able to increase the longevity of their species' members greatly with the discoveries of new medicines, and improvement in healthcare, along with the self-education of their species.

Human beings have now begun to wonder whether it is possible to push death further away, and whether a person, who can live forever, could be engineered. Human beings are also surveying other planets, millions of miles away, on which they can settle if their own planet, Earth, is no longer able to support their existence.

Human progress has its cost. And success produces hubris. An unintended consequence of the rapid advances in technology and faster economic growth is the destruction of Earth and its systems which nurture human existence. Evidence of inexorable warming of the planet, which will make human existence, as we know it, not possible for much longer, has raised alarm bells. People are beginning to doubt this paradigm of progress that is producing rapid advances in the standard of living and longevity of human beings. Daring capitalists, like Elon Musk, are financing the development of rockets to carry people into space. Rich people who can afford it are already booking their tickets for the journey.

Yuval Noah Harari tells a story in his masterful account of the evolution of humans' capabilities—*Sapiens: A Brief History of Mankind*. An American astronaut, training for a mission to the moon, meets an old Native American. The Native American asks for a favour. Would the astronaut deliver a message to the spirits who live on the moon? The Native American utters something in his tribal language and asks the astronaut to memorize the words, which the astronaut cannot understand. The tribal leader adds that he cannot tell the astronaut what the message is because it is a secret that only his tribe and the moon spirits are allowed to know. When the astronaut returns to Earth, he finds someone who can speak the tribal language. He repeats the words he has memorized. What the message means is, 'Don't believe a single word these people are telling you. They have come to steal your land!'

Harari narrates this story to remind his readers about the fact that the remarkable scientific and material progress humanity has made in recent centuries has a dark side to it as well. The human species is only one character in the bigger story of evolution. Other forces are also at work. They are changing the story too. To make a difference for the better, human beings must reorient their views of their place in the world, and their roles in the story. Arrogance must dissolve into humility. While we are playing clever tricks on the world around us to make it meet our needs—little jokes, as Frost says, Nature, of which we are a small part, has the capacity to play a much bigger joke on us.

My Story

After I obtained a Master's degree in Physics, I was recruited into the Tata Administrative Service. The Tata Group, founded over a hundred years ago, is legendary in India for its social responsibility. I worked with the Tatas for twenty-five years and learned the principles of good management as an apprentice to some great leaders of the industry.

In the 1960s, the Tatas decided to set up a factory on the outskirts of Pune in western India to produce trucks and buses, designed and made by Indians, to meet the growing demand for commercial vehicles in the country. The Indian economy was short of foreign currency. Whatever India needed would have to be produced in India. There was not even enough foreign currency for the Tatas to import the special machines required for the factory. Even these would have to be made in India.

Tata engineers had been schooled by engineers from the world's largest producer of commercial vehicles at the time—the German company, Daimler Benz. When the technical collaboration with Daimler Benz ended in 1969, the Tatas had to break out on their own to reduce payments in foreign currency for technical assistance. The Tatas also had ambitions to export Indian-made vehicles, even in competition with Daimler Benz, to earn foreign currency for the country.

The Government of India permitted Tatas to obtain technical

support from European companies for the design and manufacture of the specialized equipment. However, the support was limited to a short time, and was restricted to obtaining know-how, along with very limited imports of critical components. Sumant Moolgaokar, the chairman of the company, insisted that the new enterprise in Pune must be a 'learning factory' where Indians would learn to do what they had never done before—and quickly.

I was put in charge of the 'social side' of this ambitious new enterprise. My job was to find young Indians, fresh out of school and college, who were willing to take on the challenge of learning and doing something that would prove to them and to the world that Indians could build and run a complex engineering enterprise that could compete with the best in the world.

Fortunately, I had Sumant Moolgaokar as my guide. He challenged me and gave me the space to learn and experiment with new ideas of training systems and compensation structures, such as a wage system for workers in which a worker's wage would be increased whenever the worker could prove that he had learned a new skill or increased his proficiency substantially. The wage paid would not be related to the output produced by the worker, because the output would be determined by whether or not there was a demand for the company's products. It was up to the management, and not the workers, to develop products the market wanted and market them effectively. The system worked. Within a few years, the productivity of Pune's 'learning factory' had double the productivity of the more seasoned factory in Jamshedpur, and it was churning out many new products to successfully take on competition from European and Japanese companies in India and abroad.

Sumant Moolgaokar loved machines, engineering and making new products. He also loved nature. He said our job was not limited to growing a body of skilled people in Pune to achieve our industrial ambitions. But it was also to recreate the natural environment around the Pune factory which had been despoiled by centuries of human activity—overgrazing by herds of domestic animals, and felling of trees for fuel and timber. In the visitor's room in the Pune factory, hung a large, black-and-white photograph of a landscape. It showed an undulating expanse of barren land, with no trees on it and hardly any bushes. A lone cyclist could be seen riding across it along a stony path. This was the land the government had given Tatas to build the factory.

Moolgaokar used to say that amongst the resources man needs, those that take the longest to grow are trees and skilled men and women. Therefore, if one wants to build a sustainable enterprise, one must begin by training people and planting trees. The training school, workshops and hostels for apprentices were operating three years before the factory buildings were constructed. This is why when the first machines were installed, skilled workers were ready.

The restoration of the natural environment turned out to be more difficult. The plan was to dig hundreds of thousands of pits in the stony soil and to plant saplings in them. The problem was that there was no water for them. The government had allocated a small number of scarce water resources only for the construction of the factory and its operation. It did not allow the usage of any of these scarce resources for the care of trees, which it considered a naturalists' fad. (This was in the 1970s, decades before environmentalism became an international movement; it was even before the Club of Rome's Report on the Limits of Growth, so the state government can be forgiven for giving greater priority to industrial development than to the environment.)

Tata hired water diviners from India and Australia to indicate sources of underground water they could drill from on the barren land. But they were not able to find any sources. Finally, taking advantage of the topography of the land, a dam was built on one end, and after a few monsoons, the natural drain-off began to accumulate into a lake behind the dam. Dr Kulkarni, an expert from the Fisheries department, was engaged to advise what varieties of fish should be seeded in the lake. Dr Salim Ali, a famous ornithologist, advised on what sorts of weeds and shrubs could be planted in and around the lake to attract birds. With the water from the lake, saplings and 'pole-plants' (long branches of trees, skillfully planted into the pits, that would sprout leaves within one or two seasons to create 'instant' tall trees) began to grow into a forest around the factory buildings.

One night, I was awakened by the company's security officer. A crowd of angry villagers had gathered near the factory gate. They said their buffaloes that had drunk water from the stream near their village had been poisoned and had died. They also claimed that effluents from the factory had poisoned the water. We gave the villagers full compensation for their animals. Moolgaokar wanted an investigation on how our effluent disposal system had broken down and wanted corrective action taken. We upgraded our equipment. Then, Moolgaokar gave the final instruction to make the system foolproof. The direction of the now fully-treated water discharge would be changed. Instead of flowing into the stream passing the village, it would flow directly into our own lake. And every month, the officers of the company and I would have lunch at the lovely little guest house by the lake, and we would be served fish caught in our own lake. We had better be sure the factory was not discharging any effluents that would harm fish or human beings!

Over the next two decades, as the factory continued to grow, employing over 10,000 people, the trees, bushes and the undergrowth around them continued to grow as well. One day, in 1986, there was an alarm. A female leopard had given birth to cubs in a dense grove of trees within the factory. The workers were startled by her appearance. The officers of the forest department were summoned and they safely removed the animals. The irony was that, of all places, the leopard had considered a man-made factory the safest place to deliver her babies!

Standing in the visitor's room, with the black-and-white picture of the land as it was before the factory came—with no buildings, and no trees and bushes—looking out towards the grove of trees in which the leopard had nestled, one could feel the wonder of a system, of man and nature, progressing together.

Systems thinking is a way of thinking, and a way of being. A way of thinking of oneself as part of a larger system, and behaving accordingly, even while pursuing one's own dreams.

Sumant Moolgaokar, chairman of Tata Engineering (now called Tata Motors) and vice-chairman of the Tata Group, demonstrated that you must first give to the environment what you intend to take from it. Industrialists usually complain that they will not invest when the country is not producing enough skilled persons for them to hire. They also want the government to give them large tracts of land to build their factories, get pesky environmentalists out of the way and remove cumbersome processes for obtaining approval of communities before building their factories. In their minds, the condition of the society around them and the environment are 'externalities', which are concerns of others, not theirs.

J.R.D. Tata, the then chairman of the group, said that whenever he had to make any difficult decision, he would first ask himself what would be good for the country, and then what would be good for the Tatas. He said that any decision that was good for the country would eventually turn out to be good for the Tatas too.

After twenty-five years with Tatas, I had to move to the United States in 1989 for personal reasons. I left with Mr Tata's blessings and support. This was before the breakup of the Soviet Union and the liberalization of the Indian economy in 1991. Mr Tata asked me to look after my family first, and to learn as much as I could from the world outside India.

In the USA, I was acquainted with some great teachers of systems thinking—Peter Senge (author of *The Fifth Discipline*), Bryan Smith (co-author of *The Fifth Discipline Fieldbook*), Charlie Kieffer, Michael Goodman, Jennifer Kemeny, and Peter Stroh (author of *Systems Thinking for Social Change*). Most of them were from MIT and they had established a highly successful consulting company, Innovation Associates, to teach systems thinking, team-building and personal mastery to business leaders. They decided to merge Innovation Associates with Arthur D. Little, and invited me to become the CEO of the company.

Soon after I moved to the US, capitalism won over socialism.

It was jettisoned after the collapse of the Soviet Union and that was 'the end of history' of ideological struggles. Management consultants now veered around to help business leaders focus on creating shareholder value, and to help investors in start-ups to create more wealth for themselves. The wealth of those who had financial capital to invest began to soar in the 'naughty nineties' everywhere, including India, whose economy had been opened up to foreign capital in 1991, with more freedom given to domestic investors too.

It seemed as if business leaders were so focused on creating benefits for their businesses that they were losing sight of the conditions of the societies in which they operated. In 2000, Kofi Annan, the then secretary general of the United Nations, rallied the governments of all countries to sign up for the Millennium Development Goals to eradicate poverty everywhere.

That was also the year I returned to India. The change in the business environment in India was palpable. The 'animal spirits' of capitalists seemed uncaged. The first few years of the New Millennium saw an unprecedented expansion of wealth at the top, and a celebration of it everywhere. Indian corporate leaders and ministers of the government approached the World Economic Forum in Davos together to declare that 'India was shining'. I, too, went with them. When the Confederation of Indian Industry (CII) hosted the closing party in Davos in 2004, I was prompted by the president of CII, who knew I loved to dance, to get the world to dance with India. So, with Shiamak Davar's troupe of lovely, young Indian dancers on stage and to the rhythm of bhangra, I stepped onto the empty dance floor and showed off my moves. Soon, dozens of men and women, in tuxedos and long gowns, began dancing as well. The young Indians came down from the stage to dance amongst them. The rich people of India and the world were dancing together—India Inc. had joined Global Inc.

In May 2007, CII invited Dr Manmohan Singh, who was the prime minister then, to its annual general meeting. He was welcomed by corporate leaders as the father of India's second freedom. The first freedom had been earned in 1947, when Indians had gotten political freedom from the British. For the next forty-five years, the Indian economy had been centrally managed and private industry had been stiffly regulated. In 1991, Dr Manmohan Singh, the then finance minister, had opened up the Indian economy and had given freedom to India Inc.

Dr Manmohan Singh took the opportunity to share his thoughts on 'Inclusive Growth: Challenges for Corporate India'. He said, 'You have all been the beneficiaries of our improved growth performance. When I read about the growing number of Indian millionaires and billionaires, about Indian companies buying multinational airports, about our clogged airports, about the real estate boom, about new holiday destinations, about soaring CEO compensations, I know that you have benefitted from the growth process.'[1]

He continued, 'In a modern, democratic society, business must realize its wider social responsibility. The time has come for the better-off sections of our society—not just in organized industry, but in all walks of life—to understand the need to make our growth process more inclusive; to eschew conspicuous consumption; to save more and waste less; to care for those who are less privileged and less well off; to be role models of probity, moderation, and charity.'

Dr Manmohan Singh invited the assembled business leaders to become the government's partners in spreading inclusive growth. He invited them to voluntarily adopt a Ten-Point Social Charter, enjoining them to invest in people and their skills, to invest in environment-friendly technologies, to be proactive in affirmative action, to adopt a corporate philosophy, which factors in the needs of the community and the regions in which they operate, and to resist excessive remuneration for themselves. He appealed to CII to develop a Code of Conduct for its members, with respect to business practices and control corruption.

---

[1] Speech given by Dr Manmohan Singh at the inaugural session of the annual national conference of the Confederation of Indian Industry on 24 May 2007 in New Delhi.

The prime minister's appeal to business leaders for ethical conduct and for concern of the whole system caused consternation amongst the business leaders. Was the prime minister suggesting that India go back to socialism? Dr Manmohan Singh told me some years later that, after that speech, he did not feel very welcomed amongst corporate leaders. They were polite but no longer warm to him.

When the then Prime Minister Manmohan Singh began his second term in 2009, he asked me to join the Planning Commission of India, which he chaired, as the member responsible for industry. Organized industry was not creating enough jobs. Businesses were complaining that it was not easy to do business in India. Government regulations were too many. Foreign investors were reluctant to invest more until Indian regulations were eased. Even Indian companies preferred to invest outside India.

The pernicious practice of hiring workers on short-term contracts to pay them less and to avoid providing them with social security, and to have freedom to hire and fire at will, had become a cancer even in the best-managed, large companies. Fifty per cent to seventy per cent of their workers were on contract. Since they were temporary workers, their employers were not motivated to invest in their development. How could the workers feel loyal to their employers when their employers had no commitment for the workers' welfare?

Industries were finding it difficult to obtain land for their facilities. Local communities objected to the pollution of their water sources, to the acquisition of their agricultural lands, and to the destruction of forests from which they obtained resources. Massive investments of billions of dollars were held up because communities did not trust businesses to look after the communities' interests. Businesses complained that it was not easy to do business in India and asked the government to explain to the people that the investments would be beneficial for the people. Here then, was industry asking the government, who they wanted to get out of business's way, to explain to the people that big corporations were good for the people! However, for the people to trust the government to represent their interests, the government would have to be closer to the people than to the corporations the people did not trust.

Dr Manmohan Singh had pleaded with CII to understand that business people must see themselves as part of a larger system for whose health they were responsible. If the people did not trust the industry because they saw the industry caring only for returns to its financial shareholders, and not for the people, the government would be compelled to regulate industry on behalf of the people, which would be resented by the industry.

According to many Indian citizens, the Planning Commission was too academic, too quantitative, and aloof from the realities of their lives. Dr Manmohan Singh, the then chairman of the Planning Commission, wanted it to reform itself so that it could be more effective in inducing more inclusive and sustainable growth of the country. Most of the big issues the country faces require collaboration between many ministries. For example, children's welfare, despite having a department dedicated to it in the Ministry of Women and Child Development, requires improvements in health systems for which there are other large and powerful ministries. Improvement of health requires improvement of sanitation and the availability of clean drinking water, which are the purviews of other ministries. Moreover, change in these matters cannot be made by the central government alone—the twenty-eight states of the country have a major role to play in bringing about changes on the ground.

Another subject of great importance to India is the creation of more jobs for its youth. This requires collaboration between the Ministry of Labour and Employment, the Ministry of Education, te Ministry of Skills on the supply side, the Ministry of Commerce and Industry, the Ministry of Micro, Small, and Medium Enterprises, the Ministry of Heavy Industry, the Ministry of Textiles, the Ministry of Tourism, and several other ministries on the demand side. Moreover, since the private sector is the principal creator of jobs, the production of people with right skills and job creation requires cooperation between the government and private enterprises. For results to be generated for the citizens, all components of the system must work together.

Dr Manmohan Singh said that the Planning Commission could not merely be a maker of plans with targets and a provider of budgets to the ministries and the states—which were its principal roles in the prevalent system. It would have to transform itself into a 'systems reform' commission, to induce all parts of the system to think together about the strategies that would produce results for the country and for more collaboration in their implementation.

He asked the Planning Commission to come up with a plan for transforming itself into a 'systems reform commission'. He also desired that it applied more systems thinking while preparing the next plan for the country. Therefore, systems thinking was used in preparing scenarios for India's development, albeit on a pilot basis, for the twelfth five-year plan. A blueprint of new capabilities the Commission had to develop to play its role as a systems reform commission was also drafted. This fed into the charter of the new National Institution for Transforming India (NITI Aayog) with which the next government, under Prime Minister Narendra Modi, replaced the Planning Commission.

Systems thinking and an ethical orientation are necessary for good business management. Systems thinking and collaborative action amongst stakeholders are essential for governments to induce changes in systems that will produce more inclusive and sustainable growth. People working in the development sector, who do not have the authority and the resources that governments and businesses have, and yet want to induce transformation of systems to create more sustainability and equity, need systems thinking even more. Moreover, concepts of a 'good organization' as a controlled system, which may work well in the business sector, cannot apply to the development sector where the boundaries of the enterprise must be more open. Networked forms of cooperation systems are essential to produce systemic change in the development sector.

The Book

Transforming Systems is about systems thinking, ethics and networked organization. Going back to my granddaughter's question, there is a bit of fiction in this book about reality. It is a collection of stories about people who have realized they must reorient their thinking about their roles to make the world better for everyone.

These are real people. A young management consultant. A successful CEO of a large company. A young woman who took a path not usually taken when she graduated from business school to work with people in the slums of an Indian city. The CEO and the director of international networks in an international NGO. A highly successful young AI developer in San Francisco, and his friend, a graduate student in cultural psychology. An Indian who returned to his country to 'give back' after making a lot of money in technology enterprises in Silicon Valley. A teacher of economic development who joined him to set up a new school for development studies in India.

It has been my privilege to converse with many wonderful persons like them from many countries in the past few years. Though the names of the persons in the stories are fictional, their questions and views are real. They are all searching for a new paradigm. They are searching for the difference with which to make the difference—the story of many wonderful people today. The questions I have, and the few answers I have learned that I would like to share with my readers, are expressed with the help of these people.

The sustainable development goals, which citizens of all the countries are aspiring for, form a stage in the larger story of humanity. The SDGs provide a backdrop for these stories. I hope readers will recognize some of their own concerns and questions on their minds in the stories of these persons' search for a new paradigm of thought and action to make the world better.

The chapters in this book are divided roughly into four parts.

The divisions are not sharp—they are permeable. To the reader, the ideas in the book will appear to flow back and forth between the parts. This is because they are part of a system of ideas and cannot be separated too sharply from each other.

The four sets of inter-related ideas are:

- Part A: Aspirations to improve the world
- Part B: Search for a new paradigm
- Part C: Reorienting our minds
- Part D: Becoming a leader

The world is changing very fast because of humanity's own actions, such as the development of new digital technologies and artificial intelligence (AI). Meanwhile, other changes, some as reactions to these technological changes and others caused by social, political and economic forces, are combining with large-scale environmental change to make the future much less predictable than it was in the previous century.

The shelf life of knowledge has become much shorter than it used to be. Therefore, patterns of learning must change—from the acquisition of information and new ideas in schools and universities early in life, to lifelong learning.

The book recommends three orientations required for anyone aspiring to make the world better:

- Systems thinking
- Ethics of citizenship
- Deep listening

In addition to these foundational disciplines, I also explain concepts of collaborative, networked organizations, which are essential for producing systems changes.

I am aware that readers of this book will be at different stages of learning about systems. Some may have become aware that a different way of thinking and acting is required to produce better and more sustainable outcomes, but may not have encountered concepts of systems thinking and networked organizations so far. For these readers, questions like why they should learn about systems thinking, and how it is different from the ways they think now, is paramount, before they venture further to learn the essence of systems thinking. They may find the earlier parts of the book, about 'aspirations to change the world' and 'search for a new paradigm' particularly useful to read before they delve into the latter parts.

Other readers, already clear about why they must strengthen their ethical orientation and become better at systems thinking may find the first few chapters not as useful as the explanations of ethical foundations and systems thinking which begin from Chapter 7.

People can learn their entire lives. As my mother, who was 98 years old when she passed away, said, 'As long as one is learning, one is living.' She was much more interested in adding life to her years than adding more years to her life. Even towards the end, she continued to inquire what was happening in the world around her and why, and to read and write in her diary.

As my mother used to say, looking at her garden, that there is nothing new under the sun—the same ideas appear in other forms. We can have greater understanding of what they are when we continue to observe and learn.

Inspired by her, I continue to learn and write. I hope the ideas in this book will be useful for readers who intend to make the world better for everyone and wish to find more purpose in their own lives.

PART A
Aspirations to Improve the World

1

The Purpose of Our Lives

Sumit turned the key, pushed open the door, and switched on the light in his apartment. Past midnight, it was Saturday morning already. It had been a very busy week. He put the key of his new Audi on the table by the door and instinctively looked at his smartphone. Many emails and messages had filled his inbox since he had left his office at 7 p.m.

He noticed a WhatsApp message sent a few minutes earlier, along with a photograph. It was a selfie of the five old college friends whom he had met that evening. There were four men, Sumit amongst them, with beer mugs held high. The fifth was a woman, holding up her smartphone, taking the selfie. The message said, 'Good to meet you guys again. Priya here.'

Sumit smiled to himself. It had been a fun evening after a hard week. All five of them had studied at the country's best management institution. The five of them used to hang out together quite often at the institute. The four men had met each other many times since. They had arranged to meet that evening because Priya, whom they had not met since they had all graduated, was going to be in Mumbai. It had been good to meet again and talk about the good times they had spent at the institute.

The four men worked in Mumbai with consulting companies and MNCs and were paid well. Sumit had clearly done the best. Still a bachelor, he lived in a well-furnished apartment in a new building, with concierge services and a gym. His new Audi was safely parked in an underground garage. The other men were recently married. They lived well too.

Priya was different. She had been amongst the top of the class, as he had been. However, she had taken a road less taken by the graduates of their institute. She had joined an NGO in Pune that was working amongst poor urban communities. She earned much lesser than what he and the others did.

Sumit woke up around eight the next morning. He made himself a cup of coffee and settled down with it in his balcony. The maid would come a little later to clean up the apartment. He went through his pending mails and responded to the urgent ones. He again looked at the photograph of the five friends taken last night.

The week had been quite hectic. Sumit was a senior project leader in an international strategy consulting firm. He had been hired on 'day zero' of the placement process, when the institution allowed the most prestigious employers to make offers to the very best students. He had done well in the consulting firm that had hired him, rising faster, in salary and responsibilities, than most of his peers who had joined with him five years ago.

On Thursday, his consulting team had made a final presentation to the client of the project Sumit was working on. Their client was a large and successful Indian company. In addition to their immediate client in the firm—the chief strategy officer—the CEO of the company was also present. Senior partners of the firm in India were part of the meeting, and a senior partner had flown in from New York as well. The three days before the final presentation had been hectic, with rehearsals, last-minute searches for more data and reordering of materials that the partners wanted. As the project leader, Sumit had to get it all done. He had slept less than five hours each night during the run-up to the final day.

The presentation had gone very well. The chief strategy officer had seemed satisfied—he had said the CEO had accepted their recommendations. His firm's partners had also seemed pleased. They had thanked him and his young team for the work done. They had hinted that they expected to get more 'follow on' work from the client, which would bring in a large sum of consulting fees.

On Friday, Sumit had been informed about his annual salary review. He had received a large increase on top of the high salary he was already being paid. He had tried to find out what raises his peers had got. Not just to satisfy himself that he was being treated 'fairly', but also to assure himself that he was ahead of them.

The five friends had not talked much about their salaries on Friday evening. Four of them, working in the corporate and consulting sectors, were doing very well—it was evident from their lifestyles. The men had felt awkward asking Priya about her salary. From her descriptions of where she lived and how she travelled, she obviously earned much lesser than they did. However, she had not seemed unhappy about it. She had seemed content with her life and with what she was doing.

Sumit thought back to the times they were together in college. Students used to talk a lot about what they intended to do when they left college. Mostly, it was the same—getting into a prestigious company, or a high-tech start-up, and making a lot of money. The placement system of the institution was geared to help them down this path. The institution, too, wanted them to get higher starting salaries, as it wanted to remain higher on the ranking list of management institutions. The starting salaries of students was a major criterion for ranking institutions. Higher-ranked institutions would attract the best undergraduate students. This is why highest-paying employers were given special hiring privileges by higher-ranked institutions—for example, 'day zero'. The firms competed with each other to become most attractive to students by offering them better monetary prospects, thus propelling young students with a desire for higher compensation levels.

It is difficult for a young person to resist the great force of this whirlpool. Sumit had never given it much thought. He was fixed upon, just like everyone, he thought, to make the most money. And why not? But now he wondered what had enabled Priya to stay out of the rat race. What did she care most about in her life?

Later that morning, he sent her a message. 'Thanks for the

photo, Priya. It was great meeting you. Would love to meet you again. Let me know when you come to Mumbai. Sumit.'

As Sumit began to wonder what Priya cared about more than making money, he began to wonder what he himself cared about. He had never bothered himself with this question. He had just chased what everyone around him was chasing. The race was to stay ahead of them. Those ahead of him were more successful. However, what were they all running towards? What was the purpose of working so hard 24/7, struggling to find a balance between their work and lives?

His aim had always been to make a lot of money, like the partners in his consulting company, who earned bonuses in millions of dollars. Some young partners drove luxury BMW and Mercedes saloons. The partners who were more senior even owned holiday properties in other countries. However, money was perhaps not all he wanted. He also wanted respect from his peers in the management fraternity, and that would happen if he climbed up to become the CEO of a Fortune-500 company, or an even larger one someday. Besides, he could make a lot of money as a CEO too.

The next week was a relatively easier one at work. The next phase of the project was being figured out by the firm's partners along with the client's chief of strategy. He had more time to reflect on where he was heading in life. He wondered what the partners—who were his immediate role models—cared about most in their lives? What about the CEO of their client's firm? He seemed driven to improve his firm's profits and to increase its value to its shareholders. Was that all that kept him awake at night? Or were there other things that concerned him even more?

Oh, well. He could not ask the CEO for a chat, as he could ask Priya, though he would have loved to find out what he cared about deep down.

- Are you falling behind in the rat race?
- What do you care about most in your life?

2

Redesigning an Airplane While Flying

Ravi was a successful CEO. His company was frequently cited in business journals as a well-managed company. Ravi's picture had also appeared on the covers of many business magazines. He was a popular speaker at business seminars. His company's stock was often recommended by stock market analysts as a stock to buy and hold. He was a distinguished alumnus of one of Indian's best management institutions and management students aspired to be recruited by his company. He was a role model for them.

He settled into the rear seat of his BMW saloon and the chauffeur drove off. The quarterly call with analysts had gone well. His team had anticipated the usual questions about pressures on margins, effects of recent regulatory changes, anticipated increases in sales, and earnings guidance for the next quarters. However, it seemed to Ravi that some young analysts wanted to show off their analytical prowess. They had tried to point out inconsistencies in the calculations. Despite the minor interruptions, his team had been on top of their numbers.

He picked up a business newspaper from the neat pile placed beside him on the seat. The story of alleged malfeasance in a large financial services company continued to unfold on the front page. Other stories of corporate frauds and fugitive CEOs who had escaped from the country were now relegated to inside pages. The editorial page had an article about the failure of corporate boards generally, and their independent directors; in particular, to prevent such breakdowns in corporate governance. The paper included the mandatory page with long lists of stock market prices and their movements. Inside it was also a full-page sponsored splash about corporate social responsibility (CSR). It had a photo of several corporate representatives in a discussion about CSR, along with some stories about their companies' CSR activities. Ravi noticed that one of the companies whose CSR activities were highlighted had been in the news for many months when local communities had protested against the pollution of the water and soil caused by its factory in their area.

The thought that there seemed to be two worlds that were not connected with each other running parallel struck Ravi. One was the world of analysts and the stock market. The other was the world in which other people lived. People in the stock market world did not seem to be concerned about the other people. Ravi remembered a cartoon by R.K. Laxman, whose cartoons had been appearing on the front page of India's largest selling daily for many years. In this cartoon, Laxman shows two beggars squatting at the foot of the stairs to the Bombay Stock Exchange. Two portly stockbrokers are descending the stairs with ear-to-ear grins on their faces. One beggar says to the other, 'Oh good. The stock market has gone up. Now life will be good for us!'

Ravi's father had worked his whole life as an officer in a large, public-sector bank. He had risen up the ranks to a mid-level position. His mother had been a schoolteacher and she had taught mathematics and science. They had brought up two children—Ravi and his younger sister, Sushma. His parents were determined to provide their children the best education they could afford. Sushma and he had studied in the best private schools, run by Christian missionaries. Both the children had learned their values from their parents, which were reinforced in their school. Honesty, simplicity and caring for others were values they imbibed. They understood the importance of hard work and striving for excellence.

Both his parents had retired some years back and lived in a

modest house his father had bought in Delhi, with the help of a loan from his bank when he was working. They had small pensions, and his father also had some investments in mutual funds from which he obtained a small supplemental income. Sushma was married. She worked with a think tank in Delhi, and lived with her husband, who was an officer in the central government in another part of Delhi.

His parents lived comfortably, albeit simply. They said they did not lack anything. His father owned a small Maruti car, which he drove himself. They visited friends and their relatives occasionally. Both loved music, and they went to classical Indian music soirees. His father was now over 75 years old, and his mother was not too far behind. They had a part-time help at home. They liked to live independently. However, their bodies were ageing and needed more visits to doctors. 'To the garage, like my old car', his father would say repeatedly to whoever asked how they were and laugh at his own joke. Sushma kept an eye on them. Ravi would drop in to visit them whenever he travelled to Delhi. And they would come to stay with him in Mumbai once a year around Diwali or New Year when Ravi could take some time off from work.

Ravi had made his parents proud by being selected for admission to an Indian Institute of Technology (IIT). These prestigious institutes had been set up by the Government of India, in collaboration with the best international engineering colleges in the world, including MIT in the USA, in the 1960s, to provide young Indians with excellent education. The IITs have become the most sought-after institutions in India for post-school education. Thousands of young people compete in a rigorous selection process, and the best of the best are selected.

After graduating from the IIT, Ravi sat for another competitive examination. This time, it was for admission to an Indian Institute of Management (IIM). These institutions for postgraduate education were set up a few years after the IITs, once again in collaboration with the best international management schools. Students from the IITs competed for admission to the IIMs The admission funnel narrowed further. The best of the best young Indians got through. Ravi was one of them.

The IITs were set up principally to produce engineers for industry, whereas the IIMs taught marketing, finance and other management subjects. The career trajectories of the best Indians who joined the IIMs were transformed—from shop floors of industrial companies to better-paid positions in marketing and finance, consumer companies, advertising companies and banks. Big companies would show up at the campuses of the IIMs to aggressively hire the best Indian talent to grow their businesses. That is how Ravi had landed a position as a senior management trainee with one of the most admired consumer goods' marketing companies in the country, where he did very well.

Ravi's son was studying computer science at Cornell University in the US. His daughter was planning to study design in New York. His schoolmates believed that Ravi had done very well in life.

When Ravi was diligently studying in school and at the IIT, he had no vocation in mind. He simply did his best at whatever he was expected to do and competed with his peers to the best of his capabilities. He had done so throughout his life. He hardly paused to reflect on the point of the race, and the purpose of his life. But recently, he was compelled to do so at a meeting of CEOs he attended.

Ravi was appointed the CEO of his company when he was 45 years old, with much fanfare in the media because he was considered very young to be a CEO of a large, prestigious company. Soon after, he was invited to a special meeting of selected CEOs organized by the Confederation of Indian Industry. The meeting was to discuss what business leaders could do for India. It was conducted by an international management consultant who specialized in the development of leaders in business.

The consultant started the meeting with a brief fifteen-minute presentation about the forces shaping the world of business internationally, and the internal and external forces India must contend with in its quest for sustainable, inclusive and faster economic growth. Then, he asked the twenty-five CEOs, who had assembled, a question—'What do you care about most in life?'

He asked the CEOs to silently think about this for a couple of minutes. He prompted them to visualize what the world around them would be like if what they most cared about became more evident in the world.

Ravi remembers the meeting very well. The silence went well beyond the couple of minutes they were allowed. Many CEOs, including him, began writing notes on the pads placed beside them. After a while, the consultant asked them how they felt about those few minutes. Several of them said that they valued the time, albeit very brief, to reflect on a profound question they hardly ever asked themselves amidst the commotion in their lives.

The consultant wondered if they would like to talk to the other CEOs on their round table regarding what they cared about. Ravi recalls that they had all gone around the table and had listened to each other. Then, the consultant asked if they had any observations to share. All said that they appreciated the opportunity to talk 'heart-to-heart' with their peers. They noticed that they all cared about their families and the condition of communities. They were also concerned about persistent poverty and inequities in the country. Some added that they cared about making their companies forces for universal good.

What followed is vivid in Ravi's memory. A participant interrupted and said that no one had been truthful. When asked why, he said that no one had admitted that what they cared about most was making more money, which was what they really did, according to him. There was a reaction from others. They said, 'We must speak for ourselves. Do not cast aspersions on our honesty.'

Ravi remembers the incident vividly, mainly because he was stung by the accusation, as many others were. Yes, he could not deny that he liked making more money. Why not? And he liked being respected for leading a company that was loved by investors and business analysts. But money and respect from his business peers were not what he cared about most deeply. He cared a lot about the happiness of his children, his wife, and his old parents. Poverty, signs of which he could see around him every day and stark statistics of which the consultant had presented at the opening of the meeting, troubled him. He would have liked to do much more to improve the living conditions of the poorest people of the country, and to give their children hope for a better future.

Since that thought-provoking meeting, Ravi had redoubled his efforts to keep a balance between his work life and his family life. However, he had not been able to do enough about the condition of the society. He was a champion for the CSR programmes of his company. However, they seemed to be only frills attached to the business operations of the company to attract public attention, whereas the thrust of the business operations was squarely to produce more profits and value for investors. Recently, the Indian government had passed a law requiring all companies to spend 2 per cent of their net profits on CSR. His company easily met that requirement and had been spending more than that even before the law was passed.

The more fundamental question that the law had skirted around was how a company made its profits in the first place. What impacts did a company's products and production processes have on the health of people and the environment? What impacts did the company's business practices have on the fabric of the society? For example, how did it treat its small suppliers, and how did it expedite the regulatory clearances they needed? In other words, the concern should be with how 100 per cent of the profits were produced, and not whether or not the 2 per cent of the profits had been spent on CSR.

The consultant in the CII meeting gave a definition of true leadership. He said, 'A leader is he or she who takes the first steps towards what he or she deeply cares about, and in ways that others will wish to follow.' Leadership begins with caring for a cause and a commitment to it. It is unlikely that there will be deep passion if one is merely complying with objectives set by others. A leader is the one who takes the first steps towards what the leader is committed to, even if they are risky steps. He does not wait for others to test the water.

Without followers, a leader cannot be a leader. Persons in high positions and with authority over others, like CEOs, ministers and generals, can make people follow them, with carrots and sticks, even when people do not subscribe to the goals the person has set. They are loosely referred to as leaders of their organizations. But what about people like Mahatma Gandhi, whom millions followed even if it meant making great sacrifices in their own lives? Gandhiji had neither official authority over his followers nor did he have any means for financially rewarding or punishing them. Yet, millions followed him voluntarily because they knew he cared for what they cared for—the freedom from various political, social and economic oppressions.

This was a very powerful definition of leadership. Ravi had returned to it many times since that meeting and wondered what he should do about what he most deeply cared for, which was affirmed in his mind when the participants were provoked by the challenge from one of them. As the CEO, he cared about the performance of his company and for the returns produced for investors. In fact, it was his duty. However, he cared for something even deeper—to make the world better for everyone, not just shareholders. And especially to make the world better for the least privileged people.

Ravi realized that, in a humble way, what he cared about was also what Mahatma Gandhi had cared about. And as the CEO of a large corporation, he had command over large financial resources, which Gandhiji did not. So, he wondered what was coming in his way to take the first steps towards what he deeply cared about. Why could he not direct the resources of his company to make the world better for everyone?

He thought again about the call with the analysts. CEOs have to account to many people, not just themselves. They have to comply with regulations and reporting systems. They are an integral part of a large socio-economic system, with many institutions interlocked with each other—corporate laws, stock market regulators, etc.

They cannot decide what purpose the corporation should fulfil in society on their own.

The challenge was like redesigning an airplane in flight. If the change in the design of the propellers got ahead of the corresponding change required in the design of the wings, the plane would crash and take down everyone in it. Therefore, whoever in the system decided to take the first steps to make a radical change would have to carry others along.

When Ravi came home, he seemed very preoccupied. 'A penny for your thought,' his wife asked. 'Making profits is easy; changing the world is hard,' Ravi said to his bemused wife. It was a statement Ravi had heard somewhere. But he couldn't remember where.

- How does one keep one's feet grounded in current reality while shaping a new reality one wants to create?
- How can one change a system of which one is only a part?
- How do you redesign an airplane while it is flying?

3

What You Care About Deeply

The bus had departed from Mumbai for Pune early in the morning. It came out of the crowded city onto an expressway, travelling past many miles of habitats untidily transforming from rural to urban along with the growth of India's economy. Buildings in various stages of completion scarred the land. When the road began to ascend gently towards the peaceful hills of the Western Ghats, with fewer signs of India's economic progress, Priya relaxed in her seat. She enjoyed long journeys because they gave her time to reflect and read. She liked reading good books.

She had V.S. Naipaul's *India: A Wounded Civilization* in her lap. Though she did not like Naipaul's acidic views on India, especially in his earlier books, *India: An Area of Darkness* and *India: A Wounded Civilization*, she admired his mastery of the English language. She felt he deserved the Nobel Prize for Literature that he had recently won.

Naipaul had written the book she was carrying in 1978, and there was a passage about young Indians building India for the twenty-first century. In fact, it was the only expression of Naipaul's hopes for India's future in the book. Coincidentally, Naipaul wrote this passage after his first (and perhaps only) visit to Pune. In the book, Naipaul describes his journey from Mumbai to Pune. He had travelled by the Deccan Queen, the fabled train, which was the best way to travel between the two cities before the expressway was constructed in the 1990s. He described the same scenery that she was passing by, as it was then, with his masterful use of words.

> But then Mumbai faded. And swamp was swamp until the land became broken and, in the hollows, patches of swamp were damned into irregular little rice fields. The land became bare and rose in smooth rounded hills to the plateau, black boulders showing...

She could see the majestic boulders now. No more badly constructed and ugly buildings. Naipaul's passage goes on to describe the young people he encountered in Pune.

> They say they are building for the twenty-first century. Their confidence in the general doubt is staggering. But it is so in India: the doers are always enthusiastic. And industrial India is a world away from the India of bureaucrats and journalists and theoreticians.

Priya had grown up in Pune. Her father had worked in one of the many modern factories that were growing around Pune when Naipaul had travelled there. Priya had gone to St. Mary's School in Pune, an all-girls school. She did very well in school, academics, debating, and sports as well. She was also the Head Girl of the school. Priya was then selected for the Economics Honours programme at St. Stephen's College in Delhi. This was the most prestigious undergraduate programme in India. After India's Independence, graduates of the college were selected in large numbers into India's top civil services—the Indian Administrative Service (IAS) and the Indian Foreign Service (IFS)—and went on to occupy top positions in the Indian government. Amongst the courses offered by St. Stephen's, Economics was the most sought after, especially since the 1990s, when the Indian economy was thrown open to international trade. Earlier, Physics had been the most difficult course to get admission into, when the Indian government was promoting the study of science and engineering to build India's own industrial capabilities. When Priya applied for admission to Economics at St. Stephen's, she was competing with the best students from schools all over India. Her admission was a recognition that she was the best of the very best.

After obtaining her Honours degree, Priya had applied to one of the IIMs. The best of the best Indian students seek admission in these institutions because they offer a fast track into lucrative jobs in the corporate sector. The premier public services—the IAS and IFS—have become less attractive than the private sector since the 1990s. Private sector salaries have shot up with the liberalization of the Indian economy after 1991. Earlier, top-level private sector salaries had been pegged by law to be comparable with top-level salaries in the public sector (which were quite low). Admitted into an IIM, Priya had been on the highest level of academic achievement so far that would position her in a high-paying job in the private sector.

What Priya was returning to in Pune, after the get-together with her four IIM friends in Mumbai, was a job which paid much less than what they were getting in the private sector.

Words of her favourite poet, Robert Frost, in *The Road Less Taken,* crossed her mind. Frost says:

> I will be saying this with a sigh
> Somewhere ages and ages hence:
> Two roads diverged in a wood, and I--
> I took the one less travelled by,
> And that has made all the difference.

Priya had always been a high achiever. Best in school, best in college—where she was a star debater and topped her class. Amongst the best at IIM too. Then, what had turned her away from the beaten track?

In college, Priya began to feel an intellectual dissonance with the Economics course. What she was being taught seemed too abstract and unreal. Macroeconomics was riven with esoteric mathematical equations. The equations were attempts to predict the behaviour of very complex economic systems shaped by the interactions of diverse people. To make the mathematics easier, the basic constituent of the system, its basic particle—a human being—was presumed to be a rational, self-interested person.

Her observation of reality around her (and in her)—how her friends took decisions and how she did too—told her that this presumption was wrong. Human beings have emotions. They very often act 'irrationally', moved by passion rather than abstract calculation. Priya sensed that economics was going in the opposite direction to physics. Physicists were trying to go deeper into the composition of matter, whereas economists were busy building grand theories on faulty foundations of what motivates human beings.

Priya could handle the complex mathematics as well as others. She could also build a logical case as well as anyone. Therefore, she was a good debater as well. She did very well in college. She topped her class, even though she was not convinced about the practical utility of what she had learned. She expected that business management would give her more useful knowledge and so she applied to an IIM, hoping to discover what she wanted to do in life after her formal education was over.

The IIM was much more nuts and bolts than Economics in St. Stephen's had been. She hung out with Sumit, Rohan, Ankit and Guri a lot—the four friends she had reunited with that evening. All four were engineers from IITs, as were a majority of students at the IIM. They ribbed her sometimes about the fuzzy stuff she had learned in college. However, she could easily keep up with them in classes on finance and marketing, and she also took optional courses in human resources, which the guys were not interested in.

She discovered that her four friends focused only on what they had to learn and what they were supposed to do. They hardly read any books whereas she enjoyed reading good books, fiction as well as non-fiction. They said they had no time to read but she suspected that they were not very interested in anything outside their academic courses. They began to use the language of rational management outside class too. 'Let's get the facts first'.

'Be objective'. 'What's the "value" in this?' 'What "returns" do you expect for your efforts?' 'Have you computed the risk in what you are doing?' They seemed to be getting closer to, or at least they talked more like, the 'rational and self-interested' persons that economists said all human beings were.

All students were expected to intern with some organization in the break between their two academic years. Students hankered for internships that would look good on their resumes when they were interviewed by potential employers. Many companies offered internships to attract the best students, ones they could also consider for potential employment. Internships with attractive employers were much sought after.

Amongst the internships on offer for Priya, there was an invitation from an NGO in Pune. Priya was attracted to it because it was different from the others, and also because it would enable her to spend a few weeks with her parents. It was this internship that set her on a path that was hardly chosen by students of IIMs As Frost writes, she:

> (Then) took the other, as just as fair,
> And having better claim,
> Because it was grassy and wanted wear.

4

Searching for a Better Way

When she completed her MBA programme, Priya joined the NGO she had interned with. It was an organization working in the poorer neighbourhoods of Pune, assisting communities to improve their health, education and livelihoods. It had been working in these areas for over twenty years when Priya joined them five years ago. Now, it was preparing to celebrate its 25th anniversary, combining the celebration with a fund-raising drive. Priya had gone to Mumbai to source potential donors.

Its office was in the neighbourhood it worked for. On a board over the unpretentious entrance to its office, in a tired building in need of repairs, was its name: The Pune Community Welfare Sanstha.

Priya came to work on Monday morning. Ms Usha Gore, the founder of the sanstha (i.e., the 'organization'), was already in the office. She greeted Priya, who put her backpack on a chair, and sat down in front of Usha across her small desk. The walls of the room were covered with charts containing numbers—of people who had attended medical clinics, women enrolled in self-help groups, children immunized, etc. Behind Usha was a framed picture of Mahatma Gandhi.

'How was your weekend? And how was your visit to Mumbai?' Usha asked Priya. Priya told her about the three meetings she had with potential donors. She reported that they had seemed interested and she had given them the information they had asked for. They had then told her that they would let her know soon what they might like to do to support the sanstha.

Priya was hopeful because none of them had said 'whether' they would support them. They all had said 'what' they might offer. Her pitch to them was for financial support to keep the organization going and to help it grow. They liked the NGO's model and seemed very appreciative of the results they had produced so far. However, they wanted to know exactly what their funds would be spent on—would they support the beneficiaries, or would they be paying for the members' overheads? One of them wanted to know how much they were charging the beneficiaries for services they provided, and whether the NGO took any share of the profits of the self-help groups. Another, while congratulating Priya for her generous spirit, tried to figure out how much salary she was getting!

'I am so glad you are with us, Priya,' Usha said. 'I used to find discussions with funds-providers very difficult. They have a model of an enterprise in their head, which is so cut-and-dry and mechanical, compared with the fluid, organic way in which we have to work. You can understand what they are saying, and you can talk to them in their language.'

When she had joined the sanstha to help Usha organize it better, Priya, too, had difficulty in understanding Usha's colleagues. The model of an enterprise in Priya's mind, taught to her at the IIM, was not the same model they had in their minds. 'Cross model' conversations are always difficult.

She remembered a discussion with Renu, the second-in-command in the organization, who was responsible for running the large community outreach programmes. Renu worked with heterogeneous teams—a few paid staff of the sanstha, several young volunteers, who worked part-time, and several members of the community who took up roles and responsibilities in the programmes. Priya mapped the various tasks that were to be performed to make a programme effective. She then selected the persons who had to perform these tasks. She felt there was a need to sharpen roles and responsibilities around organizational functions, such as communication, training, delivery of services, etc., and to lay down some performance measures. She gave due weightage to each role and placed the paid staff into salary bands so that they could be 'fairly' paid in proportion to their skills and contributions.

Renu was uncomfortable with this scheme. It meant bringing in more management discipline. But it would also change the spirit of the organization. People would be required to comply with their job definitions and with management's expectations of their performance, whereas right now they happily did whatever was required of them without any discussion of whether or not it was their job to do so, because they were deeply committed to the purpose of the organization and the cause it served. They cooperated with each other and respected each other. There were very few occasions when Renu had to intervene to resolve some disagreement. She appreciated the desire to 'professionalize' the organization to make it more effective, but she was concerned that, with everything being converted into written rules, the organization would become too bureaucratic.

Discussions with Renu made Priya appreciate the fundamental difference between an organization motivated by commitment and an organization managed by compliance. She recalled the speech of Mr Muthuraman, CEO of Tata Steel, delivered at the institute. Tata Steel is legendary in Indian business as an organization with great human values. Priya and the other students studying human resource management had heard him keenly. Mr Muthuraman had shocked them by declaring that the 'professionalization' of human resource management was killing the spirit of human organizations. He had said that HR managers devise precise measures of performance, objective appraisal systems and systems of compensation that sought to justly reward measured performance. However, in the process, they smother the innate desires of people to do good and to improve themselves. He had eloquently explained what Renu was trying to. The students had applauded him but had promptly forgotten what he had said. They had known that if they wanted to be hired in the HR function of a large firm, they would be expected to be very good at those very same 'professional' processes of HR management they were being taught at the institute, which Mr Muthuraman seemed to deride.

In the institution, they were taught the fundamental difference between Theory X and Theory Y of human resource management which Douglass McGregor had propounded. Theory X says that human beings intrinsically dislike work and shirk responsibility, and therefore, need formal direction and close supervision. Theory Y says that human beings have an intrinsic desire to learn and perform well, and managers should create an environment for their self-actualization. They were asked to believe that Theory Y was better. Yet, as Mr Muthuraman had pointed out, almost all the professional techniques of HR management they were taught seemed to conform more with Theory X.

The students had been introduced to some concepts from the field of organizational learning. Amongst the leading contributors to this field were Peter Senge, author of *The Fifth Discipline* (which advocated the need for more 'systems thinking') and Chris Argyris. Argyris had explained a difference between 'espoused theories' and 'theories-in-use'. He said that an 'espoused theory' is the theory an individual claims to follow, whereas the 'theory-in-use' is the theory the individual actually follows, which can be inferred from his or her actions. Thus, HR managers (and teachers of HR) may espouse Theory Y, though in practice, they follow Theory X.

Argyris also explained the difference between single-loop and double-loop learning. Single-loop learning involves improvement of knowledge and practice without changing the underlying theory. On the other hand, double-loop learning questions the validity of the underlying theory and requires the adoption of a new theory to produce the desired results. As Priya became more engaged with the sanstha and more committed to its cause, she realized she must do some double-loop' learning herself!

Shortly after she joined the sanstha, she attended a programme at the Sabarmati Ashram on 12 March 2015—the anniversary of the day Mahatma Gandhi had begun the long Dandi March to obtain salt from the sea to claim people's rights to their own land and salt, which the British had denied them. The programme was organized by a group of young business entrepreneurs who had made quite a lot of money and wanted to give back to society. They felt that progress to reduce poverty globally was too slow. They invited hundreds of young people who wanted to improve the lives of the poorest people—which had been Mahatma Gandhi's lifelong mission—to assemble in the ashram and learn from Mohammed Yunus (the founder of the Grameen Bank), Elabhen Bhat (founder of SEWA) and some other great leaders of successful poverty reduction movements. Their thesis was that if more people with motivation and energy could learn the methods these leaders had applied, the pace of poverty reduction would accelerate.

To Priya, this seemed like a wonderful opportunity, and she was setting out on a journey into unfamiliar territory that she had not been fully prepared for by her education in economics and business management. While introducing the programme to all the participants, the curator said that the objective of the programme was to enable the participants to make plans for their own journeys towards the vision they all shared—of reducing global poverty faster. He added that there would be three plans that would support each other. One would be a plan of action—what must be done when, by whom, and with what resources. The second would be a plan for collaboration. As the causes of poverty are many, a number of systemic actions are required to root it out. Therefore, there must be a plan for systematic collaboration. It was important to consider who to partner with to obtain the support needed, and who to support in the efforts towards the same cause. It was important to seek out such partners because lofty goals could not be achieved alone. The third plan, he said, would be a plan for one's own learning—what must one learn to improve one's own ability to achieve the required goal. It was important to put down the questions for which answers were needed. Then, a plan had to be formulated for whom to learn from and regarding the source of the knowledge. Lastly, milestones had to be set for what to learn by when.

Action-oriented managers are accustomed to review progress against action plans. To change a complex system, one has to collaborate with others, many of whom may not think alike. The curator said that some double-loop learning was necessary. Priya liked the idea of a learning plan very much. She began to maintain a journal in which she noted her own 'theories-in-use' she felt she must question.

Here are some questions from Priya's journal:

1. **What is the difference between organizations designed for commitment and organizations designed for compliance?**
Both Renu in the sanstha and Mr Muthuraman when he spoke at the institute, had suggested that formal, 'professional' organizations seemed to be designed to ensure compliance with the organizations' goals, and therefore, the spirit of working voluntarily for a cause a person was committed to was smothered in such organizations. So, how should an organization be designed and how should it operate to maximize the energy of commitment?

2. **What forms can an organization adopt to enable coordination?**
An organization structure is required to enable the coordination of many actions within the organization to produce a collective outcome. Hierarchies enable coordination. A higher level is required in the organization to ensure that actors at the level below them are aligned. Then, another level of supervision is required for the coordination of people at a higher level. And if there are many people at this next higher level, another level may be required. Thus, large organizations end up with large hierarchies.

If several organizations whose efforts must be coordinated to achieve a large outcome, such as reduction of poverty, are independent of each other as they are very likely to be, then who will be the overall boss? And how will they efficiently coordinate with each other without a boss?

3. **How can one apply more 'systems thinking' in practice?**

The discipline of systems thinking, Senge had pointed out in *The Fifth Discipline*, is essential for addressing many complex systems problems facing mankind today—environmental degradation, climate change, persistent poverty and increasing inequalities in societies. Before one determines the right action to improve the condition of a complex system, one should understand the relationships between the diverse forces that together compose the complex system.

The managerial instinct is to break down a system into parts quickly, without understanding the connections amongst them. Then, separate people are assigned responsibilities to fix the separate parts. This seems like a logical thing to do, to get people to focus, and to ensure they are accountable. However, this causes actions within 'silos', which very often compete with each other, waste resources and hampers the production of the overall outcome that is desired.

People have begun to espouse systems thinking in government, private sector, and even in NGOs. However, their theory-in-use, which is evident in how they continue to address big problems—by breaking them down into component problems, with each component assigned to a dedicated group with expertise to solve it—shows that the theory-in-use is not systems theory.

4. **How can one 'scale up' results in the social sector?**

The tendency is to scale up the organization and its resources so that results can be scaled up. Whenever asked how the organization is doing, the first response is to say how large the organization has become—how much its budgets have grown over time, how many people are on its rolls, etc. Social sector organizations are supposed to make improvements in the conditions of societies. What they must scale up are the results produced outside themselves, not their own size.

How would one rate two social sector organizations—one of which is twice the size of the other but produces the same results as the other? Is the larger organization the better organization, more worthy of respect, or the smaller one?

5. **How can one attribute results achieved in social change to any of the diverse partners who have collaborated to produce it?**

Since outcomes of social change, such as improvement of health of citizens or increase in incomes from livelihoods, are produced by collaborative action in a complex system, every partner's contribution must count. How much credit should be given to each?

This question is asked when the organization asks for financial support. Donors want to know what outcomes will be produced by the money spent. They expect to see a direct, measurable link between the inputs of the organization and the final outcomes in society. This is an example of the conflict between linear thinking and systems thinking.

6. **Who are the leaders in a system?**

Who leads an organization? The person on the top? Or are others in the organization also leaders in their spheres of work? Especially when they are counted on to do whatever is required because they are committed to the cause, and their roles are not laid out in detailed job descriptions with rules they must comply with. In a hierarchical organization, leadership may be concentrated in a few positions at the top. In less formal organizations like the sanstha, leadership must be dispersed and exercised even by front-line workers in the field.

Going beyond organizations to systems, the question of who leads becomes more intriguing. How should leadership be exercised in partnerships between diverse, independent organizations that must cooperate to make change in complex systems, and by whom?

Priya had found a lovely description of a leader in a book she often referred to. She had found the book in her institute's library, and now had her own copy of it. Its title was *Leading Beyond the Walls*, with the subtitle: *How High Performing Organizations Collaborate for Shared Success*. The book, produced by the Drucker Foundation, is a compilation of essays by many famous thought leaders in business, management and public policy. In this book, Jim Collins, the author of *Good to Great* and *Built to Last*, (books Priya had also read) says, 'You are a leader of and only if people follow you when they have the freedom to.'

Collins' insight about the essence of leadership resonates with the definition of a leader provided by the curator of the remarkable meeting at the Sabarmati Ashram in March 2015. He said, 'A leader is she or he who takes the first steps towards what she or he deeply cares about, and in ways that others wish to follow.'

7. **Was she really listening to people who had views different from hers?**

The curator had provided a structure of a journey plan for a person who wished to make a change in the world and develop her own leadership ability. If requisite leadership abilities are not developed, change in the world will not be produced. The curator had insisted that the change plan must include a learning plan to guide the change-maker's own learning.

Lately, Priya had begun to appreciate how difficult it was to understand, and even to listen to another person with a different world view. Usha had mentioned the difficulties she had faced in being understood by financial donors, as well as the difficulty in understanding them. They seemed to live in different worlds. Renu and Priya had different mental models of what an organization was and different theories-in-use of what was required to make an organization work.

Priya was observing how often conversations between people turned into conversations between stereotypes, rather than conversations between people who wanted to understand each other. People boxed each other under labels, such as 'corporate sector types' and 'social sector types'. Social sector types would 'expect a corporate sector type to say that' and vice versa. There was very little effort to get to know the real person behind the stereotype and to understand what the person was really saying, rather than what the person was presumed to be saying.

Poor listening seemed to be the root cause for most misunderstandings. Good listening to people unlike oneself was essential to understanding complex systems, which had to be seen from many viewpoints to be understood completely. Good listening to others, to appreciate what they deeply cared about, and to understand their theory-in-use, was also essential to improve collaboration between diverse people working towards a shared aspirational goal.

In her notes, has put down better listening as a capability she must cultivate on her learning journey.

Three plans are necessary to lead change: an action plan, a plan for collaboration, and a plan for learning.

Priya's questions:

1. What are the differences between organizations designed for compliance and organizations designed for commitment?
2. What forms can an organization adopt to enable coordination?
3. How can one apply more 'systems thinking' in practice?
4. How can one 'scale up' results in the social sector?
5. How can one attribute results achieved in social change to any of the diverse partners who have collaborated to produce it?
6. Who are the leaders in a system?
7. Was she really listening to people who had views that were different to hers?

5

How Will AI Machines Learn Ethics?

David felt on top of the world. From his apartment's window, towards the east, he could see the Berkeley hills across the San Francisco Bay; towards the north, glimpses of the yachts in the Sao Saulito harbour; and westwards, the Golden Gate Bridge. Property prices in San Francisco had risen faster than all other cities in the US in the last ten years, with the tech boom in the neighbouring Silicon Valley. His small apartment, with its amazing location, was worth over two million dollars. He was thirty years old. Yet, he could afford it.

David worked in an AI laboratory. AI had become the most exciting field in technology. Amongst the thousands of well-paid technology developers swarming around San Francisco, working in the sprawling campuses of the world's most admired technology companies in Silicon Valley, and wanting to live in the exciting San Francisco, he felt that both his work and life were the best of the best.

David had a very attractive girlfriend—Jenny. She lived in Berkeley and was doing her PhD at the university there. He spent many weekends with her, driving through the vineyards in the Napa and Sonoma valleys in his BMW coupe, and dancing in cafés and bars in San Francisco and Berkeley.

David's parents, who lived in a suburb of Phoenix, Arizona, were conservative people. His father had served in the US Marines.

His mother had been a schoolteacher. David was their only child. He had studied computer science at the University of Austin in Texas and was considered a genius in his class. He was hired on campus by a Silicon Valley technology company, where he worked alongside the best of the best from other technology schools—MIT, Carnegie Mellon, Stanford, Cornell, amongst others. Many of his colleagues were Asians—Chinese and Indians who had been to these great American schools too. Indeed, it was a team of the world's best talent. David was considered the smartest amongst them. He worked on the most cutting-edge technology challenges. His employers were keen to hold on to him and his compensation grew very fast.

Moral questions about whether technology was making the world better for everyone, and what the purpose of his work and life was did not engage him much. Sometimes Jenny would tease him about this. 'You are a good guy,' she would say. 'Don't blame yourself for it. But what do you think about those poor guys on the corner holding up placards saying that tech companies are causing homelessness in San Francisco?' David would shrug her question off with, 'It's the market at work. I am paid more because someone wants to pay me more, because they want what I can do. I offer to pay more for an apartment I like, and the landlord is willing to sell or rent it to me because he wants the money. No one is forcing anyone in the market to do anything against their will. If some people are paid much less than others, it must be because their work is much less valuable.'

One Sunday morning, when they were having coffee in their favourite garden café in Berkeley, she handed him an article in *The New York Times* that she was reading.

The title was 'When Robots Have Minds of Their Own'. It was written by Cade Metz. Metz had reported a conversation with a researcher in OpenAI—the AI lab in San Francisco founded by Elon Musk. Metz said, 'The (researcher) showed off an autonomous system that taught itself to play Coast Runners, an old boat-racing video game. The winner is the boat with the most points that also crosses the finish line. The result was surprising: the boat was far too interested in the little widgets that popped up on the screen. Catching these widgets meant scoring points. Rather than trying to finish the race, the boat went point-crazy.'

AI is enabling machines to do almost everything human beings can do—they beat humans in complex games and they can drive cars through traffic. Nevertheless, researchers find that machines need human guidance to tell them what the purpose of the game is. Intelligent machines can go berserk. 'In some ways, what these scientists are doing is a bit like a parent teaching a child right from wrong,' says Metz.

David agreed with Metz. AI programmes have to be trained. 'How do you train them to learn right from wrong?' Jenny teased him again. This time, Jenny seemed to have gotten through the protective shield David had drawn around himself to enjoy his good life and success undisturbed by the condition of the world beyond it.

He recalled a discussion about the uses of big data analytics with two friends in the cafeteria of the AI lab. They had agreed that big data analytics has three uses—targeting solutions, surveillance and advertising. In medicine and agriculture, for example, big data analytics enable very specific solutions customized precisely to fit the need. Thus, they improve outcomes and reduce waste of resources.

The benefits of big data analytics for the lives of human beings and the condition of the planet, that computers and AI programmes are now enabling, are expected to be enormous. If big data analytics and AI enable doctors to anticipate when and where a problem will strike in a body, they can also help intelligence services to anticipate when and where a terrorist might strike, provided of course, they have enough data about everyone to analyze. This is highly possible now with the ubiquity of smartphones and other Internet-enabled devices. But what if a government begins to use big data and the power of AI to monitor its political opponents? This is becoming a big concern for citizens. Clearly, the purpose to which data analytics and AI is applied is a moral question. The third application of big data and AI is money, which paid for the high salaries that the three of them enjoyed. It paid for his apartment in San Francisco, his BMW coupe, and for much else, with plenty to spare too.

This third lucrative application was selling advertising. Social media platforms, like Facebook and Twitter, offered their services for free. Yet, the companies made money—by charging advertisers a fee for obtaining access to data about the users of these platforms. Social media companies monetized the large trails of data that users left on their platforms, about who they were, what they were doing, where they were, what they liked, etc. They enabled advertisers to target people—offering them what they knew they would like, rather than wasting money in scattershot advertising to millions, hoping to hit a few birds. Looking at themselves and the other young people in the café—all of them the best of the best from the best technical education institutions in the world—one of them had joked, 'It seems the smartest people in our generation are working on this hugely important problem of how to sell more advertising!' Then they had laughed and gone back to their computers.

The question about the purpose of the enterprise, which *The New York Times* article raised, brought that discussion to David's mind again. What was the purpose of his work? What good was it contributing to?

David wasn't much interested in politics. Jenny and her family were deep-blue Democrats. David's parents were deep-red Republicans. Jenny did not discuss politics with David. She liked him and enjoyed his company. She did not venture beyond the occasional tease about how lucky he was to be able to live so differently from the people around him.

However, lately, politics had come up between David and his parents. He visited them every year for Thanksgiving and Christmas. They would say grace together before their dinner as they always had. He went to church with them when he was home, though he had stopped going to church altogether once he had left home for college.

David's mother often called him when he was in San Francisco to check on him. His parents were very proud of him, of the work he was doing, and how well he was doing. However, they were concerned about the effect the city's culture would have on their son. San Francisco was a spring of new freedoms—for blacks, immigrants, and homosexuals—if one was a deep-blue Democrat. However, if one was a deep-red Republican, it was a place where morality was breaking down. His parents were worried about the influence his friend, Jenny, would have on him. They had heard that her family, Democrats in Boston, were great supporters of the Civil Rights Movement. Moreover, the university in Berkeley had the reputation of being a fomenter of rabble-rousing, anti-authoritarian protests. This especially galled his father. His life in the Marines had taught him great respect for discipline and authority.

The run-up to the US Presidential election in 2016 deeply divided the country. Donald Trump emerged as the presidential candidate for the Republican Party, which he had recently joined, defeating a slate of opponents with strong Republican credentials. He vowed to make America great again while exhibiting great irreverence for the institutions of American democracy. He tweeted insults to his opponents in both Democratic and Republican parties. In his rallies, he incited violence against his opponents, asking his supporters to 'body slam' those who came in his way. He said that he would deport all immigrants without proper documentation. He would build a great wall between Mexico and the US. He vowed to put the Democratic candidate, Hillary Clinton, in jail if he were elected.

Trump's vision of a 'Great America' was a vision of a big bully whom everyone feared, who could hire and fire at will, as he had on his popular TV show, *The Apprentice*. For Jenny and the people in San Francisco who David knew, America was great because it stood up for the freedom of oppressed people everywhere. For them, the Statue of Liberty in New York Harbour was a symbol of America's values, not Trump.

When his mother told him that his father and she were busy campaigning for Trump, David was dismayed. He respected his parents' values. His father had worked hard as a Marine officer, sometimes in tough situations. He had provided enough for his family. A man of great integrity and with great commitment to his responsibilities, he was a rock his family could lean on, as did all his colleagues in the Marines. In the communities in which they had lived, his parents had always been considered the pillars of the community. They contributed money and time to community charities.

When Hillary Clinton called Trump supporters 'white trash', David lost respect for her. His parents were not trash. How dare she say that? Nevertheless, it did bother him that his parents would find Donald Trump worthy of their support, while he disliked Trump increasingly with every tweet and statement he made. There was something in what Trump stood for that resonated with his parents. What was it?

The messy run-up to the US elections brought the 'lords of the universe' in California—the promoters of social media companies and AI, who had become multi-billionaires—down to earth. The volumes of data these companies had about citizens, combined with the power of AI, had been illegally used in political campaigns. It was even alleged that the Russians had used the data to meddle with the US election process, and a Special Counsel had begun investigating it.

The three richest people in the world at that time were the technology tycoons—Jeff Bezos of Amazon, Bill Gates of Microsoft and Mark Zuckerberg, the young founder of Facebook. With fluctuations in the values of their company's stock prices, their rankings amongst the wealthiest persons in the world shifts. Nevertheless, they remain amongst the eight richest people in the world. Oxfam has estimated that the eight wealthiest people in the world, which also includes Larry Ellison of Oracle—another technology tycoon—is equal to the wealth of the bottom half of the world's population. In other words, eight individuals own as much as 3.8 billion people do.

The young evangelizer of the power of social media and technology, Mark Zuckerberg, was asked to appear before the US Congress in April 2018, to explain how a force supposedly for so much good in the world could be so easily misused. Not only could privacy of data be easily breached, 'fake news' and 'hate speech' could also be easily spread. There were rising demands in the US, and in many other countries too, for governments to regulate social media. In India, violence had broken out in communities, and many people had even been lynched, spurred by a viral spreading of incitement on WhatsApp—a platform owned by Facebook.

The stories of how powerful technologies were developed are inspiring. How some person with a vision, often a very young person, developed an idea, with limited resources, in a garage or in a university dormitory—as some of the technology tycoons had. And then, how the technologies spread rapidly, making their inventors billionaires. Stories of developments of new technologies never end with the projects that create them. The impact of technologies on societies become known when they begin to spread around. The more powerful the technologies, the more complicated are the next stages of the stories. The Manhattan Project accomplished its stated mission when an atomic bomb was produced at the Los Alamos Laboratories. Then, another difficult project was organized to drop two bombs on Hiroshima and Nagasaki. Stephen Walker recounts the story of this project in his book, *Shockwave*. The success of the projects stunned the world with the power of the technology that had been unleashed. Albert Einstein and Enrico Fermi, physicists who had urged the US President to develop nuclear energy, were dismayed with the use to which the new technology had been put. The leader of the Manhattan Project, Robert Oppenheimer, expressed his anguish 'over the fact that no ethical decision of any weight or nobility has been addressed to the problem of atomic weapons'.

The example of nuclear energy and the bomb may seem an egregious one while discussing the responsibilities of leaders of businesses and technology innovators. However, its exaggeration helps to bring out a critical distinction between, on the one hand, excellence in management and execution, and, on the other hand, the necessity for statesmanship to clarify. It also helps to insist upon the accomplishment of an ethical purpose for the enterprise, and not merely get things done on a grand scale.

Technology is a neutral force, albeit it can be a very powerful one. Human beings are wise to fear the consequences of the spread of a new technology. Promoters of technology are disdainful about those who suggest caution. They dismiss them as anti-technology and anti-progress. 'It always works out well in the end,' they blithely say. They turn a blind eye to the battles for regulation of powerful technologies—safety and pollution controls of automobiles, regulation of the uses of nuclear energy, even for generating clean power, clashes about the benefits and dangers of genetically modified crops, and, now, contentions about the benefits and the harms of social media platforms. Those who express concern and suggest pause are not against technology. They are simply concerned about the impact unbridled technology can have on other things that human beings value.

Social media and AI are approaching their 'nuclear' moment. They cannot be allowed to proliferate without regulation. The large technology firms, led by Facebook, offered to self-regulate the uses of their technologies. They would put their best people to develop ways to stop the spread of fake news and objectionable speech on their platforms.

David was on a crack team to find AI solutions to regulate social media. Fake news and objectionable speech seemed fundamentally different problems. Fake news was a report of something happening which had not happened. The report was made real with videos shown purportedly of the incident actually happening. AI could be used to ascertain if the video was doctored. AI could also be used to check inconsistencies in the video, or in the narrative report of the incident. However, determination of what was 'objectionable' material was much more difficult. Different people may have different views of what is objectionable. Donald Trump's hardcore supporters would cheer whatever he said, whereas his opponents would object that he was dividing people and inciting hatred.

Cade Metz, the *NYT* reporter, had observed: 'In some ways, what these (AI) scientists are doing is a bit like a parent teaching a child right from wrong.' However, different sets of parents may have different views of what is right and wrong. Would Jenny's parents have the same views as David's? They would have widely different views regarding different matters, like the rights of immigrants, for example, or respect for Muslims. If an AI scientist is expected to be a good parent to his AI child, what values will he transmit to it? And how did the parent learn his values in the first place?

AI machines have the capacity to learn. They can look into masses of data, observe patterns and make predictions based on the patterns. They can self-test their own predictions. Was the result as expected? If yes, do it again. If not, try something else, and if that works, use that knowledge again.

David knew, from being familiar with the state of the art of AI, that while AI programmes can teach themselves how to predict more accurately, they cannot teach themselves how to handle unusual situations they have never encountered. Thus, AI programmes for self-driving cars observe what a human does when an unusual combination of external conditions as well as malfunctions in the car occurs, and it builds this into its memory to use when and if it encounters a similar situation.

But sometimes ethical judgements have to be made while driving a car. If a child suddenly crosses the road, should the driver swerve sharply and risk the lives of the passengers in the car? Maybe he should. What if a dog crosses the road? Or a cow? The judgement involves values assigned to the lives of animals, children and cows. Societal values differ across societies, and they evolve and change. The ethical values an AI machine would have learned from its human parents may offend other human beings.

Moreover, societal values are not constant. They evolve. For example, women are accorded much more respect in almost all societies than they were in the same societies a hundred years ago.

Affirmative action requires that women, as well as other historically disadvantaged groups, be given equal opportunities for education and employment. Biases against women and minorities must be overcome.

A real-life example revealed the hazards in machine learning. An AI programme was developed to relieve recruiters of the drudgery of reading thousands of job applications. An AI machine trained itself to go through past records of thousands of applicants to select the best. It analyzed whom human recruiters had selected from those applicants in the past so that it could more efficiently do what human beings had labouriously done before. Not surprisingly, the AI machine continued exhibiting the biases against women the human recruiters had exercised before!

It would be very difficult to teach an AI machine to make the ethical judgements necessary to remove supposedly objectionable material. Even a committee of people selected to do this—which seemed to be the solution being most favourably considered—would find it difficult to do it justly. This is because they would have their own biases affecting their judgements.

How machines learn had been the focus of David's work in AI. He was now becoming very curious about how human beings learn, and especially how they learn the ethical and moral values that guide their conduct. He decided the time had come to ask Jenny. She was a cultural psychologist. He had often joked about the fuzziness of whatever it was she said she studied, whereas what he worked on was sharp, mathematical and practical. But now the time had come for him to explore the non-mathematical worlds of human emotions and beliefs. Perhaps Jenny could teach him something.

- How do human beings develop their values?
- How can an AI machine determine what material is objectionable and to whom when human beings themselves cannot decide the same?

6

Partnerships for the SDGs

Nancy was tired. The three-day-long meeting of the board of trustees had concluded. It was a large board for a small organization. There were fourteen trustees. Eight were women—from Japan, Bangladesh, Kenya, Lebanon, Brazil, the US, the UK, and Finland. And six were men—from India, Ukraine, The Gambia, Colombia, and two from the UK. They had flown to Hanoi in Vietnam for this meeting.

Nancy was the director for Advocacy and Network Development of an international NGO, based in the UK, working to promote the care of the elderly around the world. She had flown to Hanoi, coach class, from a meeting in Bogota regarding an emerging network of organizations in South America, who were coming together to strengthen a movement for the cause of the elderly in South America.

Nancy had been working with international organizations in the field of development for thirty years. Much of her work had been devoted to the care of children. She had lived many years in China and Africa. She had lived in her home in England only for a few years.

Her husband was an artist. They had a cottage in the countryside not too far from London. He painted in his studio while she was away, tended their little garden, and sometimes rambled around the country with his paintbrushes. Their two children were married, and they had two little grandchildren living in London. The grandchildren loved to visit their grandfather in his cottage, to play with his friendly cocker spaniel, and to wander around the country with him.

Nancy had obtained a degree in Development Economics from Oxford. She worked with the British government's international development organization for some years, and then with international charities. She loved her work. Both she and her husband, though they could not be together enough, felt blessed that their avocations were also their vocations.

She was sixty-two years old now. Her passion for her work enthused all around her. However, lately, her body seemed not so willing. It was fitting that she was now directing her passion and great experience to building an international network devoted to the care of the elderly. The cause was what kept her going.

With the board meeting over, Nancy and Henry, the CEO of the organization, were reflecting on the ups and downs of the last three days. The organization was registered as a charity in the UK. Its central office was in London, where Henry worked from. He travelled a lot too. But hardly as much as she did. Besides, he was twenty years younger than her.

At the conclusion of their meeting, the trustees had reflected on the progress made by the organization. What struck them was how far they had travelled, in less than three years, down the path to becoming a palpable network of organizations around the world devoted to a common cause. It was only three years ago, at their meeting in Delhi, that they had firmly committed to the goal of reshaping themselves into the secretariat of an international network of willing partners—what Nancy had been urging them to consider. The trustees had also reviewed the significant changes in the external environment that were making it increasingly difficult for international NGOs to operate in the prevalent model of charities based in the UK, and other rich countries, trying to improve the world.

Governments of many developing countries were not

comfortable with these NGOs. The NGOs were critical of conditions in these countries—in fact, that is why they were there, to help improve them. However, when they highlighted the citizens' unmet needs, it showed the governments in poor light to their own citizens, which reduced the citizens' trust in their government. Sometimes governments even suspected some international NGOs of having a political agenda to destabilize the government. They were very suspicious of these NGOs' foreign sources of funds.

Grants from western governments for international development, which the NGOs were drawing from, were reducing. Governments of western countries were under pressure to balance their budgets with the sluggishness of economic growth after the 2008 financial crisis. When budgets for domestic social services were under stress, maintaining assistance for citizens in other countries was more difficult.

An organization working on the cause of the elderly found it even harder to get funds when the overall budgets for development were reducing. It had to compete with funds for work on the care of children, causes of women, and environmental protection and climate change—much more popular causes in the public imagination. Besides, it was easier to make an economic case for investments in the education and health of children. The investments would pay back in future economic growth. The case for women was economically compelling too. Bringing women into the workforce makes a contribution to the present economic growth. Climate change and environmental degradation have become widely recognized as limits on economic growth. All these causes have strong economic rationales, in addition to their moral claims.

What economic value do elderly persons add to their countries' economies? In fact, they seem to be an economic burden. They have to be provided with pensions and they need more medical care than others. Their cause becomes hard to advocate when governments have to balance their budgets. The challenge of effective advocacy was one of the two challenges Nancy had taken up when she accepted the role of director of Advocacy and Networks.

The other was the challenge of shaping a network of organizations operating within their own countries that would tackle issues of the elderly in their own societies. Organizations based within their countries could understand local conditions better and could develop solutions customized to local needs. They would not be mistrusted by governments as a 'foreign hand' meddling in the country. If they learned how to, they could marshal resources locally for their work, and not have to rely on grants from rich countries, channelled through the centre in London. Such sources of funds were dwindling, and local sources of funds had to be found to support the work.

The writing on the wall was clear to the trustees in November 2015. If they wanted to serve the cause of the elderly around the world—which was their mission—they would have to change their organizational model. They would have to develop a strong international network of increasingly self-reliant organizations. The size and strength of the network would matter much more than the size and strength of the London-based charity. They would have to change the measurements they were accustomed to for assessing their performance, such as the sizes of their budgets and the number of employees they had around the world. They would have to change the agendas of their meetings to review the progress towards creating a strong network, more thoughtfully and more vigorously. The network could not just be a 'nice to have' slogan. Implementation of the concept of a network would have to become their strategy to achieve the goals of their organization. Indeed, if they did not build a strong network fast, their own survival as an organization would become doubtful.

The incoming chairman of the board had pointed out that they would have to evolve into a new form of organization: they could not just turn a switch to change their organization. Like redesigning an airplane while flying in it, it would be a risky process. If they did not change the design of their organization, they would not be able to reach their goal. However, they would not have the luxury of grounding the airplane to do its redesign. While in flight, they would have to adjust the design of many systems simultaneously and compatibly with each other—governance, resource management, people skills, the change in the role of the central secretariat in London, strengthening of regional nodes in the network, etc.

The board meeting was exhausting for Henry and Nancy because progress of redesign and change of many systems of the organization had to be reviewed. There were several moments of confusion when trustees asked why they were making the change that particular way. Some even asked why they were making this change at all—had they not got too much on their plate?

At the end of the meeting, when the board had reflected on all they had done in the meeting, and how far the redesign of the organization had progressed since 2015, they congratulated Henry, Nancy and the other directors in Henry's team. At the same time, they realized how much further they had to change to complete the redesigning of the organization into an effective network. Most of all, they would have to let go of the embedded theories in their heads about how organizations must be managed to accomplish complex tasks in a dynamic environment.

The trustees with corporate backgrounds (mostly men) had more difficulty than others (mostly women) who were working with grass-roots movements of change to accept the need for letting go control. Their instinct, which had served them very well in their corporate careers, was to seize more control when things seemed out of control, to make lines of reporting tighter, and to measure more things more precisely—to make it clear who was in charge. Even though they had intellectually understood the need to let go and to create a network, letting go was hard when so much had to be managed. 'Networks' was now their espoused theory of organization, and 'hierarchies' lingered as their embedded 'theory-in-use'.

Partnerships are essential, but partnerships are difficult

The Sustainable Development Goals (SDGs) are inspiring many people around the world. They are referred to frequently in business conferences. Civil society organizations recall them repeatedly. Government officials often cite them. It seems there is a consensus about the goals. Now the question is—how can the stakeholders work together more effectively to achieve them?

The seventeen SDGs are:

1. No poverty
2. Zero hunger
3. Good health and well-being
4. Quality education
5. Gender equality
6. Clean water and sanitation
7. Affordable and clean energy
8. Decent work and economic growth
9. Industry, innovation and infrastructure
10. Reduced inequality
11. Sustainable cities and communities
12. Responsible consumption and production
13. Climate action
14. Life below water
15. Life on land
16. Peace, justice and strong institutions
17. Partnerships to achieve the goal

None of these goals can be achieved alone. They are interlinked. Progress must be made with several goals together to enable the achievement of any one of them. For example, No Poverty (Goal 1) must go with Decent Work and Economic Growth (Goal 8) and Reduced Inequality (Goal 10). Zero Hunger (Goal 2) must go with Good Health and Well-Being (Goal 3) and Clean Water and Sanitation (Goal 6). Surely, there have to be some connections between Affordable and Clean Energy (Goal 7), Responsible

Consumption and Production (Goal 12) and Sustainable Cities and Communities (Goal 11).

The last goal says it all. Partnerships are necessary to achieve all goals. Partnerships are required between many stakeholders to achieve any goal. And partnerships are also needed amongst teams working on different goals. In fact, the seventeen SDGs should be seen as sixteen SDGs with the seventeenth as the necessary enabler, within each of them, and cutting across all of them, to enable the achievement of the sixteen.

However, partnerships working on shared goals is not the theory-in-use embedded in models of professional management. Professional management breaks complex problems into components, and then directs the requisite expertise to manage each of the components. Professionals like to accomplish what they are expected to, and they want to be rewarded for their accomplishments. Competition develops amongst teams working on the different components. They begin to compete for resources and recognition, rather than collaborating to improve the whole system.

How deep-seated is the instinct to break complex problems into parts, and then to work on each part, expecting that the system will thereby be improved, was explained to Nancy by a retired British special services officer. He had set up a consultancy to train leaders to solve systemic problems. He recalled a training programme for the partners of an international management consultancy. The task he gave them was to formulate a plan to make a city more livable for its citizens. He presented them with the facts regarding the city and the condition of its various subsystems—its transportation, water supply and sewage, health infrastructure, education, recreation and culture, systems for citizens participation in governance, etc. He explained to them that all the systems were connected with each other. They had to make the plan in four hours. Since they were thirty in number, they divided into teams of six each. Each team chose a component they felt they had most knowledge of. He mentioned that there might be a prize for the best team. 'Get on with it,' he said, 'the clock is ticking.'

The members of each team debated amongst themselves, googled for information, made blueprints of solutions and plans with timelines. They returned in four hours. Every team made a sleek presentation. Then, they turned to the consultant. Who was best?

They were shocked when the consultant said that they had failed the citizens of the city. He said that the plan for urban mobility, which was the sleekest of all the plans and the one that would be completed fastest too, would probably cause the most damage to the city! The plan presented an exciting solution for urban mobility, disregarding its impact on the city's sewage and drainage systems, and on the environment. He asked them to put the proposed urban mobility plan alongside the proposed plans for sewage, drainage, parks and recreation. The obstacles the urban mobility plan would create for other plans became apparent.

He pointed out that none of the partners had examined how their solutions would fit with others. They were all busy working within their competing silos. None of them engaged in any intermediary meetings with the other teams to adjust their plans. They did not spend any time together in the beginning, as they should have, to understand how the pieces would connect with each other. In their planning process, they did not build any requirement for consultation amongst the teams.

The metaphor of 'redesigning an airplane while flying' makes the consequences of applying a non-systemic approach to improving a complex system very vivid. If the team redesigning the wings were to put new wings on the plane before the teams redesigning the tail section and the nose had completed their work, the plane would crash.

A systems picture of the issues to be addressed, explaining the relationships amongst them, is hardly ever presented for people to understand what must go with what. Instead, what are offered are lists of important issues with goals for each of them. If there is any systems thinking and analysis done to produce the list, it is lost. Thereafter, teams and experts work hard, like the consultants in the training programme, to address their favourite causes. They may achieve their own goals, but they will not make the whole system better unless they apply more systems thinking to their work.

Deeply embedded 'theories-in-use' of how large, complex problems should be solved are not systemic in their approach. Governments, large corporations and even large developmental organizations, like the UN, do not work systemically. The UN is divided into many agencies, which compete with each other for turf and budgets, much more than collaborate with each other.

Problems such as persistent poverty and inequality, poor health and environmental degradation that the SDGs aim to solve are systemic issues. They have multiple interacting causes. They cannot be solved by any one actor. Nor are they amenable to silver bullet solutions. They require a disciplined application of systems thinking and a combination of many actions together to change the system.

- Partnerships are essential for resolving systemic issues, such as environmental degradation, persistent poverty and inequality.
- Why are partnerships difficult to form?
- How can a network of partners function without a central authority?

7

The Origins of Ethical Foundations

Jenny and David found a quiet corner in their favourite Berkeley Café. David brought two lattes to the table. He settled down in his chair and opened his notepad. 'Ready, professor, for my lecture on cultural psychology?'

David had explained to Jenny the project he was working on to develop an AI algorithm to weed out objectionable posts from social media. He had also shared with Jenny his dismay with the political views of his parents. He wondered how his parents, whom he respected greatly, had become supporters of Donald Trump. Was there any 'science' that explained how people developed their beliefs in what was right and wrong?

Jenny was happy that David was at last interested in what she was deeply engaged with. He was great company and they had good times together, even though he did not seem concerned with the things she cared about deeply—inequality and injustice, and what made people venture out of their comfort zones and safety to take up the causes of oppressed people. David was comfortable in his cocoon. She sometimes teased him about it but never went any further. He was a good guy. So, why risk ruining their comfortable relationship?

Jenny had prepared for this meeting. David said it could be the first of several tutorials. She had brought some papers with her, and she was looking forward to some deep discussions about what really mattered to both of them. Her mother had quizzed her about their relationship. Did Jenny think David was the sort of person she could spend her whole life with? Jenny knew that she needed to make a deeper connection with David if she were to consider a long-term relationship with him.

Jenny began with an introduction to cultural psychology. Cultural psychologists combine a psychologist's interest in mental processes with an anthropologist's interest in understanding the specific contexts in which people live and learn. They study how variations in context affect deep mental processes such as ethical values. She explained to David how cultural psychology might be a good field to find the answers to his questions. 'And I am at your service,' she teased David.

She had brought Jonathan Haidt's *The Righteous Mind: Why Good People Are Divided by Politics and Religion* with her. David's eyes lit up when he saw the title. This was the question on his mind. 'I brought this for you,' Jenny said, 'because Haidt explains lucidly why the rational part of the brain cannot understand its own emotional side, and how reason and faith reside in different mental worlds.'

She continued, 'Rather than throwing the whole book at you, I googled around for a good review of it. I came across a good one, which was within an essay, reviewing four other books. The title of the essay is, 'Who Will Robots and Elephants Vote For: Donald Trump or Xi Jinping?'[1]

'I was intrigued by the essay because one of the books reviewed is *Prediction Machines: The Simple Economics of Artificial Intelligence* and another is, *How Not to be Wrong: The Power of Mathematical Thinking*, by Jordan Ellenberg, which was rated by none other than Bill Gates as the ten best books last year. I thought I might get some insights into your field, AI, while you explore mine!'

'Let me explain the highlights of the essay,' she added.

To understand her analysis, first, let's look into Haidt's book,

---

[1] https://foundingfuel.com/article/who-will-robots-and-elephants-vote-for-donald-trump-or-xi-jinping-/

The Righteous Mind: Why Good People are Divided by Politics and Religion. Jonathan Haidt had studied cultural psychology at the University of Chicago. Haidt says that he obtained some of his deepest insights into the origins of moral ideas during a research project in Odisha in India, where Richard Schweder, whose work had inspired him, had earlier done seminal work in the 1980s. Living amongst people in Odisha, a state rich in Hindu traditions, with temples and pantheons of gods that people worshiped, Haidt observed two sources of moral codes—one that anthropologists explore and the other that psychologists' study. Anthropologists study the social and religious traditions through which people learn the societal 'rules of the game' they must observe. Many of these rules, for example, those concerning food and sanitation habits (vegetarianism, eating with only the right hand), relations between the sexes (marriage, adultery, etc.), relationships amongst members of families (the responsibilities of parents and children for each other), and relationships between people in society more broadly (such as the caste system in Hinduism), are considered moral codes, breaking of which invites social and religious sanctions. Psychologists and moral philosophers, on the other hand, are interested much more in the inner workings of the human mind.

Haidt provides some deep insights into the nature of moral codes.

1. Within everyone is an elephant, and also a rider trying to control it.
2. There are two types of moral codes—individualistic and socio-centric.
3. Morality has five foundations. Conservative moral codes are built on all five foundations, whereas liberal moral codes are built on two.

Haidt uses the lovely metaphor of the elephant and the rider to explain the relationship between the rational part of the brain and the 'non-rational' emotions, faiths and beliefs swirling in the mind that guide human behaviour. The elephant is a huge beast. The rider would like the elephant to obey the rider's orders. It is not easy, though. The rider must accept moving with the elephant too, or else he will be thrown off.

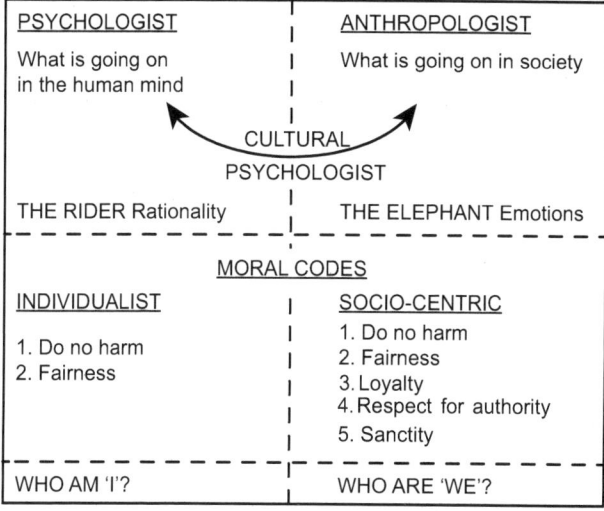

Fig 1: Understanding Ourselves

Reason and emotions

The science of economics is founded on the premise that human beings make rational decisions driven by their self-interest. Empirical observations prove that this is not always so. Therefore, economists are expanding their notions of how human beings make economic decisions. To rational intelligence, economists have now added emotional intelligence and social intelligence as intelligences that human beings use to determine the right thing to do. George Akerlof, an economics' Nobel Laureate, says that people's identities also shape the economic decisions they make.[2] Therefore, 'who' a

---

[2] George Akerlof, Rachel Kranton, *Identity Economics: How our Identities Shape our Work, Wages, and Well-Being.*

person is also influences what the person will choose to do. And 'who' a person thinks he or she is will be determined by the culture in which the person grows up.

Cultural psychologists have been ahead of economists to find out how human beings make decisions. Economists so far have tried to figure out what goes on inside the mind of the rider, whereas cultural psychologists have been figuring out what goes on in the mind of the elephant as well.

Moral codes

Haidt expands the foundations of moral codes. 'Doing unto others as you would have done unto yourself' is a golden rule of morality, founded on the principles of 'causing no harm' and 'fairness'. However, many moral codes of societies relate to actions, which an individual may want to take because he or she wants to, and which may not cause harm to anyone else. Nevertheless, such actions may not be approved in the society. For example, personal dietary preferences, such as eating non-kosher food or pork or beef are taboos in many societies and disrespect of religious symbols or the desecration of national emblems can provoke moral outrage in strongly nationalist or religious societies—even if these acts are done in private.

Haidt says that morality has five foundations. In addition to 'harm' and 'fairness', morality is also founded on the basic principles of 'loyalty', 'respect for authority' and 'sanctity'. He distinguishes between 'socio-centric' and 'individualistic' moral codes. Individualistic (or egocentric) moral codes emphasize the rights of individuals—to 'be themselves' and 'to do their own thing', whereas socio-centric moral codes are founded on other principles too.

An individualist moral code is the basis for liberal economic as well as liberal social ideologies. 'Me' values came into prominence in the 1970s, with the hippy movements in the US and Europe. 'Me' values were also endorsed by economic theories founded on notions of purely rational and self-interested human beings that came to the fore in economics around the same time. The rise of liberal ideas pushed aside deep-seated, 'old fashioned' yearnings for values of loyalty, authority and sanctity that people have.

Loyalty, authority and sanctity are socio-centric values. They honour the collective values of a group of people—a tribe, a religious community and a nation. Individuals help a group to maintain its cohesion and strength by honouring the values others in the group have. Individuals must realize that their own health depends on the health and sustainability of the society in which they live. An excessively individualist moral code can be destructive of society. This explains the visceral reaction, even hatred, that religious people and 'nationalists' have towards 'liberal' thinkers and anti-religious 'secularists' as well as anti-religious 'communists'. They see liberals, secularists and communists as 'amoral' people.

Values

Conservatives and liberals may use the same words to convey what they value. However, the concepts and meanings of the words they use can be very different. For example, both Republicans and Democrats in the US say they respect 'family values'. However, they see family values very differently, as George Lakoff, the American cognitive linguistic and philosopher, eloquently explained in 1995, in his book *Moral Politics: How Liberals and Conservatives Think*.

In the conservative model of a good family, fathers and mothers have distinct roles. Fathers must provide for the family and protect it. Mothers must care for the well-being of all the family's members. Children must respect their parents. Conservative families are caring and disciplined families. In the liberal model of a family, too, parents care for their children. But parents' roles are more fluid in the liberal model and children are given more space to express themselves and to develop in their own ways. Fairness, as well as doing no harm to others, are moral foundations for both types of families, whereas, respect for authority, loyalty to one's family and nation and the principle of sanctity (respecting religious and national symbols, for example), are stronger moral foundations for conservative families than for liberals.

Within every person is an elephant and a rider who tries to tame the elephant. The rider tries to be cool and calculating and to reason. But the elephant has a mind of its own, and feelings and moods, which the rider often cannot understand. It is not easy to have 'reasonable' conversations between people whose elephants cannot get on with each other.

David liked the metaphor a lot. 'What else?' he asked Jenny.

'Haidt had obtained his insights into socio-centric moral codes during his study period in India. So, it would be interesting to know how Indian philosophers frame moral codes. The essay I have brought for you also has a review of *Adi Shankracharya: Hinduism's Greatest Thinker*, by Pawan K. Varma.

Hinduism is a wonderful religion. It has thousands of gods and goddesses, and hundreds of thousands of temples. It is also one of the most intellectual religions in the world. The Vedas, the oldest scriptures of Hinduism, were composed in the period from 1500 to 500 BCE. They are compilations of hymns and prayers which are profound reflections on the cosmic order. Building on the traditions of the Vedas, Shankaracharya, an eighth-century AD Hindu philosopher, went further. He explored the nature of phenomena and the relationship between human thought and the universe.

'I found the epilogue of Varma's book most interesting,' Jenny said. 'Shankaracharya was an uncompromising intellectual. One must wonder how ordinary Indians, many of whom were not even literate, could relate to his vision of Hindu thought. Varma says in the epilogue, "There has been a concerted effort to somehow unite the unrelenting non-dualism of Shankaracharya with a theism that is more appealing to ordinary people craving for the grace of a personal god in their search for solace and assurance." According to Verma, Ramanuja, one of the great minds of Hinduism, who followed Shankaracharya, was keen to find a way to provide philosophical legitimacy to theism, with all its pageantry of worship and ritual and bhakti. Ramanuja understood that Shankaracharya's concepts were, "for lay devotees, much too intellectualized a construct. It did not provide the assurance that human security, need and fulfilment seek in the here and now". Further, most people need "some tangible concept of the absolute to identify with; a divinity that they can internalize in personal terms; the solidarity of faith—not in a concept—but in a deity that is comprehensible."'

Science and faith

The essayist, reviewing Haidt's and Varma's books, as well as books on AI and mathematics, comments that Hinduism's two great thinkers, Shankaracharya and Ramanuja, were thought leaders in two different domains of knowledge. One of these domains, primarily Shankaracharya's, may be accessible through the rational, scientific method, and with mathematics and analysis of 'big data'. This is the domain in which 'artificial intelligence' works. The other, primarily Ramanuja's, is beyond the realm of scientific deduction and numbers and mathematics. It becomes accessible through intuition and faith when rationality is suspended. Shankaracharya explored the mind of the rider. Ramanuja understood the feelings of the elephant.

Peter Drucker, the great management philosopher of the twentieth century, had consulted with the CEOs of the largest companies in the world, and with presidents of countries too. He said that whenever he met an important person, he would always ask for the person's opinions first, and not facts. He said that any smart person knows how to find facts that would support his or her opinions. Our beliefs determine what facts we accept, because within the human mind, the elephant is more powerful than the rider. The 'Google world' of the twenty-first century, Haidt points out, makes it much easier for the 'press secretary' to find the 'alternative facts' that will support the chief's opinions. Googling makes it easier for both, the internal press secretary within each of us as well as the president's official press secretary!

Technology sharpens divisions

A great expectation from the Internet was that by enabling people everywhere to connect with people anywhere, it would bring people closer together. However, the world has become more divided by the technologies applied by social media platforms, which give people facts they prefer and make connections for them with people they 'like'. The 'big data analysis' that empowers Google and social media platforms such as Facebook and Twitter is the knowledge of people's preferences these platforms sell to advertisers (and even to political parties, as the Cambridge Analytica scandal revealed). Thus, the elephants within us are being herded into virtual corrals, of 'people like us' separated from 'people not like us'. People within these corrals listen only to others in the same ideological corrals. They shut out the views of people in other moral and ideological corrals, even when they live together in the same countries, the same towns, and sometimes even in the same houses.

The big shock for many Americans with the election of Donald Trump was how viscerally divided Americans had become. They live in the same country and are governed by the same constitution. Yet, they have very different visions of what makes their country great. In India too, divisions are sharpening amongst people, about their visions of what will make India great. Will India, a richly diverse country, with many 'different elephants in the room', people with many traditions and many religions, be a country in which people will relish its diversity? Or will one tradition and one religion shut out the others?

'Thank you for the great lecture, Professor,', David said, and closed his notebook. 'That is a lot to think about. And thank you for the homework,' he said, picking up the essay to read. 'Let us go for a drive this afternoon and have dinner at our favourite fish restaurant in Sausalito. We will choose another date to discuss the implications of this ancient wisdom for my project.'

8

Shutting Out 'People Not Like Us'

Since his tutorial with Jenny, David had been very busy with his project to develop an AI solution for removing objectionable material from social media. He had read the essay Jenny had shared with him. The ideas she had explained provided a new lens to examine the issues his team was grappling with.

Jenny and he had gone home to visit their families on Thanksgiving. After the Thanksgiving holidays, they met in his apartment in San Francisco with the lovely view of the bay. The season had changed to winter. It was too cool now to sit out in the garden café in Berkeley. Besides, smoke from fire raging in Northern California had drifted down towards Berkeley and its neighbouring towns. The air outside was too polluted.

David opened a bottle of chardonnay and poured it in two glasses. He settled down to tell Jenny what was on his mind. He said he had three sets of reflections. One set of reflections was about the wide world in which technology companies were operating, where they seemed to have lost sight of bigger and deeper forces than the force of technology. The second set of reflections was about the ethics of technology companies. And the third were observations about the quality of conversations amongst people.

1. Living everywhere; belonging nowhere

Introducing the first set of reflections, he opened his notebook and showed Jenny a sketch he had drawn. It was a picture of the Earth, with lines going around it in circles, none touching its surface. Within the band of lines, he had drawn a dollar sign, and had written a dotcom address and the words 'neo-liberal globalization'. There was also a sketch of an airplane flying around the Earth. On the Earth, he had sketched an elephant.

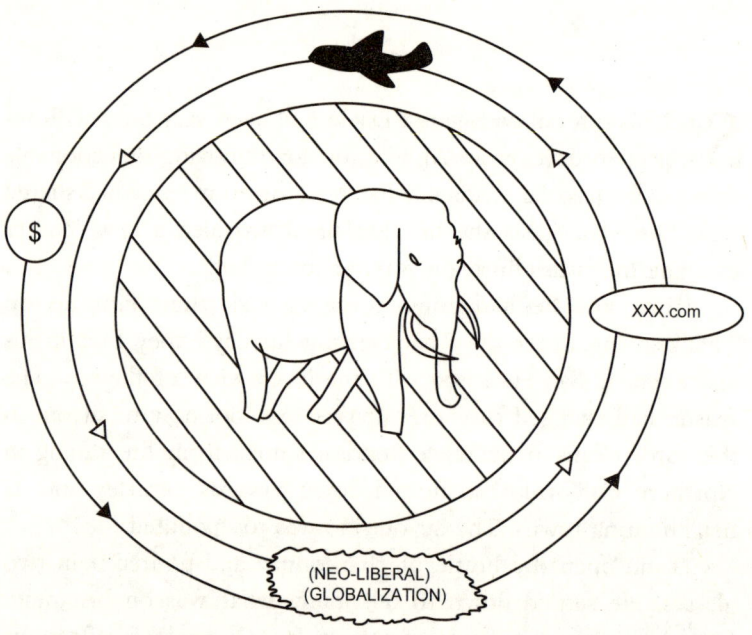

Fig 2. *Buzzing Around the Elephant Within*

David said, 'Haidt's metaphor of a rider and an elephant within each of us made me think that the world has become divided between a bunch of riders, who are connected with each other and understand each other, and a world with many elephants that these riders do not understand. There is a global community of "people like us" who can live everywhere and belong nowhere. With globalization, money flows easily. So does digitized information. This global community trades freely in money and whatever can be converted into money, and communicates easily in whatever can be easily communicated in digital form. This makes transactions amongst them efficient and knits them together. Mostly, these are good people. Whatever their religious beliefs, they follow the golden rule of fairness, of doing unto others as they would have done unto themselves, which is a fundamental rule for any trustworthy system of commerce. In addition, they do not want to cause harm once they become aware of it. However, according to Haidt, they have less value for the other social codes that matter a lot to elephants.

'These global people seem barely concerned with loyalty to one's tribe and nation. In fact, many of them consider ideas of national boundaries and identities retrograde. They say these ideas come in the way of progress towards an increasingly boundary-less world required to advance the globalization agenda. They laugh at moral codes based on faith and social traditions that would not pass modern scientific tests, such as dietary restrictions and norms of attire, whereas to many people (like my parents), such things matter a lot. From our perch, "people like us" look down upon the elephants. We think we have evolved, so perhaps the people below will too, if they're given time. We became too self-absorbed in our "liberal" world, out of touch with the values of the rest, and arrogant too. Hillary Clinton even called Trump's supporters "white trash", a very offensive characterization of people like my parents! No wonder resentment has built up amongst people around the world against their governments, who they felt were too driven by ideas promoted by an international elite. They want their governments to listen to them, and to stand up more strongly for their interests. This seems to be a big driving force behind the rise of Donald Trump. Also, behind Brexit. And behind the "yellow vests" movement that began in France at the end of 2018. Even behind the rise of many strongmen leaders outside the Anglo-Saxon world—in Russia, Turkey, China and the Philippines.

'The implication of this first bundle of thoughts, for our

project for policing social media, is that many countries will not accept a system designed and managed out of the USA. And I fear that Trump's supporters may not accept a system managed by tech companies in San Francisco. There is too much suspicion of hidden agendas, even in the US, for US tech companies to be trusted even if they had the competence.'

Jenny agreed with him. She said, 'Let me add something, which will reinforce your views. I have been talking to my friend, Reema, from India. Reema is doing research in Political Science at Berkeley. She is focused on the rise of new political movements in India since its independence from the British. You have found Haidt's framework useful in explaining the current political currents in the US. Since Haidt's research was founded on insights he obtained in India, I thought it would be interesting to ask Reema whether Haidt's frameworks would explain political developments in India as well. I gave Reema the essay I had shared with you, which had reviews of Haidt's book as well as the book on Hindu philosophy by Varma.

'Reema said the tension between the two strands of Hindu philosophy presented by Varma—the liberal, rational strand, on one hand, represented by Shankaracharya, and the conservative, faith-based strand, represented by Ramanuja, on the other—seems to have strengthened in the past four years since the election of Narendra Modi as prime minister and the rise of the BJP, his political party. India was founded as a secular country, whereas Pakistan, which was carved out of India by the British when they left, was founded as an Islamic nation. Though Hindus formed the majority in India, the Muslim population was very large too. Another large minority group was Christians. Mohandas Karamchand Gandhi, whom Indians refer to as the father of their nation, was a very religious man. He was a Hindu who respected all religions. Jawaharlal Nehru, India's first prime minister, had also read the scriptures of all religions. Though his family was Hindu Brahmin—the highest caste of Hindus—he was not a religious person, unlike Gandhi. Nehru wanted to promote a scientific, rational temperament to make India a modern country.

'Nehru and his Hindu compatriots passed legislations that overturned Hindu traditions, which they believed were unjust. For example, they changed marriage and succession laws to enable Hindu women to have property rights they had been denied earlier. However, they were reluctant to apply the same norms to Muslims. Honouring the principle of secularism, they did not want to interfere with Muslim religious traditions. It seemed the rational rider was prepared to take on the elephant within Hinduism, while it was reluctant to stir the elephant within the Muslim community. They claim that conservatives within Hinduism have resented the invasion by the Indian secular government into Hindu beliefs and traditions, while appeasing Muslims. They have successfully stirred up the Hindu elephant against India's ruling establishment, even provoking violence against Muslims.

'With the conservative side of Hinduism on the rise, there is a fight with Hindu secularists about which is the "real" Hinduism. Is it the intellectual tradition of Hindu philosophy that stayed above the rituals of all religions? Or is real Hinduism, the one propounded by the Rashtriya Swamsevak Sangh (RSS), the countrywide sociopolitical movement that spawned the BJP as a political party, which seeks to restore Hindu's pride in their exceptionalism.

'Is the real Hinduism the Hinduism of Gandhi who said "I do not want my house to be walled in on all sides and the windows to be stuffed, I want the cultures of all lands to be blown about my house. But I refuse to be blown off my feet by any?" Or is the real Hinduism the one rooted only in the truths written in the Vedas and Upanishads?'

Social media

Jenny continued, 'Coming to your project, David, Reema has shown me a story that appeared on the front page of one of India's leading English newspapers, *The Indian Express*, on 21 November 2018. As you know better than me, India is a very attractive market for the

US social media giants. With its large population, which has not yet been penetrated by social media, it is the largest market open to these companies outside the US. China, the only other country with over a billion people, has developed its own social media platforms. It is reported that WhatsApp has over 200 million active users in India, and the number is increasing rapidly. Facebook and Twitter are also growing fast.

'With the spread of social media, its unsavoury sides are infecting the Indian society and politics rapidly. Armies of trolls are reportedly engaged by organizations affiliated to the BJP and the RSS to target opponents.[3] With ruthless efficiency, they besiege anyone who opposes their ideology. There is great alarm in India about the destruction of social harmony as well as democratic institutions by the misuse of social media. So, the government has called upon the social media titans to rein in the spread of false news and objectionable speech on their platforms. Well, you probably know all that, David. Here is the amusing story in the paper. It has a picture of a tweet that Jack Dorsey, CEO of Twitter, had posted on a visit to India, where he had met with the prime minister to assure him that Twitter would remove any objectionable posts that might create trouble during the elections in India. Well, the first post he had to pull down was his own!

'Dorsey met with some women activists from the Dalit community who have been struggling for freedom from centuries of repression by upper caste Hindus. A young Dalit rights-activist had designed a poster of a Dalit woman holding up a placard that read "Smash Brahmanical Patriarchy". Apparently, Dorsey felt that it would be good for Twitter to be seen supporting the rights of women, Dalit women in particular. So, he posted a picture of himself holding the poster with the women on his sides. A flood of messages slammed the poster as "Brahminphobic". A government officer tweeted that the picture has the "potential of causing

---

[3] *I am a Troll: Inside the Secret World of the BJP's Digital Army*, Swati Chaturvedi, Juggernaut Books, 2016.

communal riots" and is "a fit case for registering a criminal case for attempt to destabilize the nation!" Twitter's legal head apologized, "We should have been more thoughtful. Twitter strives to be an impartial platform for all. We failed to do that here."

On social media and Indian TV, several people said that the CEO of an American company, a stranger to India's culture, had no business to comment on it.'

'Fools venture where angels fear to tread!" David remarked and added, 'We high-flying techies in the US are strangers in India, and we are becoming strangers even in our own land!'

2. Ethics of technology

'My second set of reflections is about the ethics of high-flying technology and social media companies,' David continued, glancing at his notes. 'When social media was introduced to the world, early in the new millennium, its promoters said it would enable people everywhere to express themselves. They professed it would strengthen democracy. The Arab Spring uprisings against dictatorships in the Middle East, which spread through social media, seemed to endorse their claims. According to its founder, Mark Zuckerberg, Facebook would enable everyone to be truly themselves. They could reveal their true selves to others anywhere in the world—their preferences, their concerns, their hobbies and their intimate photos, too, if they wished to. Thus, they could build large communities of friends, of people who liked what they liked too. Access to Facebook was free—it was a service to mankind.

'The service was free for the innocents posting information about themselves. But Facebook charged advertisers fees for accessing personal information about them. They could make their advertising effective by targeting their advertisements very precisely to "markets of one", saving the huge costs they would otherwise incur on broadcast advertising on TV and billboards, hoping that many people would be attracted to what they were offering to sell. "Markets of one" are very attractive for politicians too. Political machines can send tailor-made messages to individuals. Big data along with AI analysis has put great commercial and potentially even political power into the hands of tech companies. Their enormously wealthy CEOs are feted everywhere. Presidents and prime ministers meet them. I saw Narendra Modi, India's prime minister, in Facebook's campus, looking very pleased with himself after hugging Mark Zuckerberg. The unintended consequences of the world-improving technologies unleashed from California began to emerge as they spread. But the technologists had not understood how societies are shaped and how the human mind works.

'The Internet and social media bombard us with millions of bits of information, messages and tweets. It is difficult for anyone to stay in touch with everyone and everything. If we try, we suffer from "attention deficit disorder". Our minds become confused and cannot understand anything. So, we must choose who we will pay attention to—the people will follow on Twitter and the friends we will have on Facebook. We instinctively stay with people we like because they are like us. If we have to make more effort to understand something or someone, we just shut them out. Thus, we get locked within "conceptually gated communities". Across the walls are others in their own resonance chambers, just like we are, hearing what they like and listening to who they like. Some lob hate bombs at the people across the walls, trolling them and viciously attacking them.

'Wael Ghonim, the Internet activist who had helped spawn the Arab Spring in Egypt with his Facebook posts, said (in an interview in October 2016 with *The World Post*) that the structure of social media promotes "mobocracy" not democracy, and that "it brings together people with common passions irrespective of whether they share is the truth, rumor or lies". He insists that "while social media was seen as a liberating means to speak truth to power, now the issue is how to speak truth to social media". Rather than uniting people, the power of technology is dividing people. Surveys report that in 2017, 47 per cent of people in the USA thought social media was bad for democracy and free speech. By 2018, the proportion had increased to 53 per cent. This was reported very recently by Russia TV, which may make one wonder whether this is "fake news" and if those numbers are right or wrong. Concerns about the pernicious effects of social media on society are growing. Within fifteen years, social media seems to have turned from the great saviour of democracy and free speech to their greatest enemy! This must be hard on the egos of these technologies' creators. It has also begun to hurt their wealth. Investors fear that more penalties will be imposed by governments around the world, that growth will stall, and that the fixes required may be very costly.

'The social media and technology giants facing the heat now were not set up to fulfil public purposes. They are private enterprises set up to monetize new technologies and to create wealth for their investors. Who should their managers be accountable to? Investors or to the public at large? CEOs of these enterprises must face many ethical issues. Even employees working in the companies are awakened to these issues. Some are protesting that they do not want to be associated with any misuse of data against civil liberties by any government. Employees at Google have protested its links even with the US government. Investors on the stock market, on other hand, seem to only care about possibilities to make more money. When Facebook seemed to be making a breakthrough into China, with some deal with its government, its stock price rose. There does not seem to be a digital solution to ethical dilemmas. Perhaps there are some fundamental principles one could apply when there is an ethical dilemma. However, would these principles be applicable in all cultures? If not, then how does one stay true to one's own values while respecting others' values? It seems to me that one must rely on an ethical orientation, rather than a standard set of ethical rules.

'An ethical orientation is essential for people who have greater power than others, whether from their greater wealth, greater knowledge, or greater political power. There is demand all over the world for people with good management and technology skills who can get things done efficiently. That is what got me up here, in this two-million-dollar apartment above the poverty down below, which you often tease me about. How can it be ensured that people undergoing training to become successful and acquire greater power, in schools of management and technology for example, develop this ethical orientation? It seems to me that, like doctors who must take the hippocratic oath, an ethical orientation should be an essential requirement for people who are given "the license to operate" the great technologies and management skills they learn. I wonder, what is this ethical orientation? And, also how can one develop it?'

3. Listening

After pausing for a little while, David continued, 'Moving to my third set of reflections, the question, which is greatly exercising people in technology companies, is how would one ensure that no objectionable material pollutes the Internet and social media? To do this, one should know what is objectionable, and to whom, which the leaders of these companies are quite clueless about, as even you showed with your story of Dorsey in India. Clearly, the solution cannot be only a technological AI fix. AI machines learn by observing how human beings respond in complex situations. So, if an AI machine must learn to manage this dilemma, human beings will have to, repeatedly, show them what to do. The problem is that human being do not seem to know how to, which is why we are in this mess.

'Testifying before the US House Committee on Science, Space and Technology, on AI, Fei-Fei Li, chief AI scientist at Google Cloud, explained that while algorithms that drive AI may appear neutral, the data and applications that shape the outcomes of those algorithms are not. She said, "(AI) deep learning systems are bias in, bias out."[4] Shannon Vallor, the philosopher at Santa Clara University, whose research focuses on the philosophy and ethics of emerging sciences and technology, has been engaged by Google

---

[4]*Wired* magazine, December 2018.

Cloud as a "consulting ethicist" and agrees with Fei-Fei Li. Vallor says, "There are no independent machine values. Machine values are human values."

'Many points of views must be considered to determine if a post is objectionable. Therefore, many diverse persons must be brought together. The need for some sort of committee to establish the guidelines and to oversee the screening process is necessary. However, the problem will be with the composition of the committee. It cannot be composed of only in-house persons, or even persons seen to be friends of the company. They will not be trusted by the public to make unbiased judgements. Diverse people representing many cultures must be in this committee for it to be credible. Conservative views, liberal views, European views, Asian views, feminine views, etc.—all must be represented. Following Haidt's metaphor, many "elephants" must come together. How then will they understand each other's perspectives and come to an agreement about what is acceptable and what is not? The last two paragraphs in the essay you gave me have really got me thinking. Let me read them to you.'

He then pulled out the copy of the essay Jenny had given him. She could see that he had underlined many parts of it. He read the last two paragraphs to her.

'In a democratic society in which citizens want individual freedom and resent any dictatorial power over themselves, but want social order too, the citizens must be able to reconcile their diverse preferences amongst themselves. Therefore, a good democracy cannot rely only on vertical processes of democracy, of voting upwards to choose the leader they want. Because then the elections will divide them along the lines of the type of society and the values of the leader they choose, as has happened in the US, and is happening in many democratic countries in Europe too. Good democracies need sound lateral processes for deliberations amongst citizens, for people to listen to each other and come to agreements about the fundamental rules of the game they will accept. A dialogue amongst people must be a dialogue amongst the elephants within us. It cannot be limited to debates about facts. Elephants must also understand each other's beliefs. Haidt suggests an antidote to the self-righteous indignation, aggravated by social media technologies, that is messing up discourse amongst people. He says, "If you want to open your mind, open your heart first. If you have at least one friendly interaction with a member of the 'other' group, you'll find it far easier to listen what they are saying, and maybe even see a controversial issue in a new light."[5]

David put down the papers he was holding. A breeze had cleared the smoky haze outside. The sun was setting and the sea had darkened to a deep purple, with sparkles of golden-red sprinkled on its surface.

'Let's take a walk,' he said to Jenny. 'I will tell you about my conversation with my father at Thanksgiving.'

We need to listen to 'people not like us'.

- Why don't we?
- Why is it hard to do?

---

[5] Jonathan Haidt, *Wired* magazine, December 2018.

PART B
Search for a New Paradigm

9

Learning to Listen

David held Jenny's hand as they strolled.
'I am very curious about what your father and you discussed. Do tell me,' Jenny said. It was chilly. David suggested they return to his apartment. The sun had set. The sea was dark. The golden-red sparkles had vanished. Instead, lights on boats in the water and in homes along the shore brightened the scene.

Once at home, David refreshed their wine glasses and began to tell her about his Thanksgiving homecoming.

'When I reached home on the eve of Thanksgiving, a political storm had broken out. President Trump had angrily labelled a judge, who had stayed an executive order on immigration—an "Obama judge". Supreme Court Chief Justice John Roberts publicly objected that there were no Obama judges, Trump judges, Bush judges or Clinton judges. President Trump fired back, "Sorry, Chief Justice Roberts, but you do have Obama judges."

'My father shocked me that evening by saying the president was right! There he goes again, I thought. How can my father be so blindly loyal to a man who seems to be tearing our country apart? What are my father's values? Usually, a remark like that would invite a sharp riposte from me. I would immediately cite other things the president had recently said or done, and sarcastically ask how a president who did such things could be a good president. And we would then begin throwing examples and counter-examples at each other to prove whether or not Donald Trump was good or bad for America. On this occasion, much to the relief of my mother, who could get very disturbed by these father-son disputations and who did not want our Thanksgiving dinner to be spoiled, I paused. I mentally repeated what my father had said. He had not said Donald Trump was a good president for America. He had only said that, in this instance, the president was right.

'I asked him, with genuine interest, why he thought the president was right. My father then told me that every human being—and that includes every judge, even in the Supreme Court—has deep beliefs. Such beliefs are not easily changed. That is why there is so much competition between conservatives and liberals to ensure that someone with the same deep beliefs be appointed as a justice on the Supreme Court. It was not the judge's loyalty to Obama, but his loyalty to the values Obama represented, that the president was calling out. I had to admit it—my father was right. I decided to tell him about the project I am working on, and the difficulty I anticipated in having a bunch of people with diverse views to come to agreements about what would be acceptable views to express on social media. These people would have deeply held beliefs, which would be different to others' beliefs. In fact, it was necessary to have diverse views to ensure that there was no bias in the group's decisions.

'How do you think one can ensure that deliberations amongst these persons do not break out into disputes about which sides they are on?' I asked my father. This was the first time I had asked him for any advice regarding my work. He seemed touched. "I don't know son," he said. "But I do know that unless we improve the quality of public discourse in our country, we will not be a great country, and I must admit, the president is not setting a good tone for it." That was when I recalled the words from the essay: "Good democracies need sound lateral processes for deliberations amongst citizens, for people to listen to each other. If you have at least one friendly interaction with a member of the 'other' group, you'll find it far easier to listen to what they are saying, and maybe even see a controversial issue in a new light." Could it be, I wondered, that rather than being so focused on the algorithms AI programmes must adopt, we should be concentrating on changing the patterns of conversations amongst people?

'Communication has two sides to it—speaking and listening. If there is no speaking, there can be no communication. And if there is no listening, there is no communication because nothing is received. From school, we are taught how to improve the speaking side of communication—how to express our thoughts more clearly, in speech and in writing, how to make effective presentations, how to give powerful speeches, and how to win debates by overpowering the opposition. We are not taught how to stop the windmills in our minds, and to concentrate on what could be going on in the mind of the other person. We don't really "listen" to each other. We only "hear" others—the words they use and the facts they offer to support their arguments. Even before they have finished speaking, we are ready with counter-arguments and counter-facts to win the debate. I realized that I hardly ever pause to ask the other person *why* they believe what they do. Actually, I do quite often. But my question is generally asked sarcastically, like saying "How could you be so stupid to believe this?".

'Good listening requires not only attention to the words, but also curiosity about *why* a person is feeling compelled to say what he or she is saying—especially when what they say sounds stupid to us. When I asked my father *why* he believed the president was right, without any hint of sarcasm and with genuine interest in why a person who I have respected so much can come to a different conclusion than me with the same facts, he felt encouraged to explain his views. And so, I learned something. He gave me a good insight into our justice system. And I also began to have more respect for my father. There are many prizes given in schools for proficiency in the speaking side of communication—for the best speaker, the best writer, the best debater, etc. There are no prizes for the best listener. I think there should be.'

'You are onto something profound, David,' Jenny said.

'Practising good listening can improve the health of the society, just as the practice of good breathing can improve the health of our bodies. Listening seems such a simple thing. One may wonder how something so simple could tone up something as complex as a society. Breathing is a simple process too. In fact, it is the first thing a baby learns to do when he/she is born. Our bodies are very complex organisms, with many complex systems in them. What I am learning in my yoga classes is how something as simple as good breathing can tone the entire body—its respiratory systems, digestive systems, and even the mind.'

Three levels of listening. Listening for:
1. **What** is the other person saying?
2. **Why** is this person convinced about what she is saying?
3. **Who** is the person speaking—how did she develop her beliefs? What is her history?

10

Shapes and Sizes of Systems

Nancy woke up and pulled open the curtains in her Hanoi hotel room. The board meeting had concluded last evening. The trustees had departed to the various countries they had come from. She would fly to Lebanon on Sunday evening to meet the team in the newly forming Middle East node of the international network for the care of the elderly. In her role as Director of Networks and Advocacy, she travelled all over the world. Her mind was very willing, but her body was weakening. She was sixty-two years old—no longer a spring chicken.

She decided to take it easy over the weekend. After a leisurely breakfast, she set herself up by the pool under the palm trees. On the table next to her, she placed a book she had begun to read on her long flight to Hanoi, along with her notebook and a pen. This would be a good opportunity to gather her thoughts.

The Asia node of the network was doing wonderful work in Vietnam for the care of the elderly. She had accompanied the trustees to attend a meeting of an IGSHG (inter-generational self-help group) in a village around three hours from Hanoi. The leaders of the group were the elders in the village. Many of them lived alone, their children having migrated to the cities for work, some leaving their children in the village to be taken care of by their grandparents.

All over the world, the numbers of older people are increasing.

With growth of economies, better sanitation, increasing incomes, and improvements in healthcare, people are living longer. Increase in longevity is proof of the success of economic development. In 1950, 34.3 per cent of the world's population was below 14 years of age and 13.7 per cent was over 60 years old. By 2017, according to the UN, the proportion below 14 years had reduced to 25.9 per cent, and the proportion above 60 years increased to 23.2 per cent. The UN projects that by 2030 the world will be older—23.7 per cent will be below 14, and as many as 30.5 per cent will be over 60.

In 1950, there were 868 million children in the world below the age of 14. Their numbers have increased to almost 2 billion by 2017. These children need education, nutrition and healthcare, and must be prepared to support themselves. Therefore, the care of children and their preparation for the future is a major thrust of government policies in most countries as well as international development programmes.

However, in 1950, there were 216 million persons older than 60. By 2017, their numbers had swelled to 962 million. Who would be there to care for them when their bodies aged, as they inevitably would, and they could not support themselves? Connections between generations within families are becoming weaker, with children moving away for work to support themselves and their children. Government budgets in developing countries are squeezed to provide just enough even for children. And, in more economically developed countries, with pressures on governments to balance their budgets, resources are constrained to continue social security and pensions for the elderly, whose numbers have increased.

Several times in the board meeting, the chairman pointed at the need for better systems thinking for developing effective strategies for the care of the elderly and their integration in societies. Nancy had begun reading about systems thinking. The book next to her was Peter Senge's *The Fifth Discipline: The Art and Practice of the Learning Organization*.[6] Senge explains systems thinking—which he

---

[6]Doubleday, 1990.

refers to as the fifth discipline. The book had become a bestseller when it was first published in 1990. Many people had bought it. CEOs proudly displayed it in their offices. But very few actually read it. In fact, the book was described by one reviewer as the most purchased and least read management book of that time! Nancy had bought a copy then—in fact, it was the one that was with her now. She had not read much of it so far. With systems thinking entering the board's lexicon, she decided it was time to look into it again.

Henry, her CEO, interrupted her thoughts. 'May I join you?' he asked. He had also decided to relax after the board meeting. 'Of course,' she said. He too had brought a book. She could not see what it was because he had put his notebook on it. Henry was an avid note maker.

While Henry was speaking, Nancy had made some notes for herself. She was noting 'what' he was saying. And she was also noting some questions for herself. What had made Henry so convinced about what he was saying?

Henry, though twenty-five years younger and less experienced than her, was Nancy's boss. She liked him a lot. He was about as young as her own son. His wife was a professional designer. He had a very young family. Their children were as young as her grandchildren. He travelled around the world a lot and was not able to spend as much time with his family as he wanted to.

Henry was a gentle, yet determined young man. He wanted to make the world a better place, just as Nancy did. He was also open to new ideas. He had studied Development Economics in Oxford, the same subject Nancy had studied many years before him. He had also worked in the same international children's charity she had, albeit in another part of the world. When the board of the international organization for elderly persons they both worked with now was on the lookout for a CEO to take the organization onto a new trajectory, they picked Henry after an external and internal search for the best candidate.

Henry noticed Nancy' book. Systems thinking was on his

mind, as it was on Nancy's ever since their board chair had begun to introduce the concept in their meetings. 'Interesting that we are both thinking of systems. What are your thoughts?' Nancy asked Henry.

Sizes and shapes of systems

Henry opened his notebook. He said, 'A principal characteristic of a system, it seems to me, is that a system has a shape. A system's properties lie in its shape, not in its size.'

Nancy was curious. 'Say more,' she nudged him.

'Think of this,' he said. 'It is not the overall size of the population that is causing stress in older people, it is the shape of the population. When the proportion of older persons increases within a population, no matter what its size, inter-generational dynamics change, and result in the problems that we are grappling with. Singapore, with a population of only 5 million is experiencing the stress of having many older persons, with too few younger people to support them, which China, with a population of over one billion, has begun to experience too. When the parts of a system go out of balance with the other parts, the shape of the system changes, and so it begins to experience ill ease.'

Noticing the puzzled look on Nancy's face, Henry offered, 'Let me give you a clearer example. One cannot gauge the health of a human body merely by measuring its size—its height or its weight. A human body is healthy when all the organs within it are working harmoniously with each other. A very small person might be healthy if her internal system is functioning well, whereas a much larger person may be much less healthy because his internal system is disturbed. Another example is the size of the economy. Increasing the size of an economy and growing its Gross Domestic Product (GDP) gives no guarantee that the economy will be a healthy one. Inequality may increase within an economy creating many societal tensions while its size increases. Larger size economies do not always result in better societies, just as the largest person may not be the healthiest. One must look inside the system, at the relationships amongst its parts, to know whether it is a healthy system. The obsession with size as the principal measure of their success can produce bad effects in organizations. I have attended many meetings of large, international NGOs in the past year when they introspected the exposes of their poor governance that came to light and damaged their reputations. NGOs have a drive to "scale up". Their intention is to increase the scale of outcomes. Instead, the scale of the organization itself becomes the objective. Organizations proudly talk about their own scale—the sizes of their budgets and staff—and how much these are increasing year on year, and the visibility of their brands. Countries are ranked by the sizes of their GDPs, and organization by the sizes of their revenues. If revenues are not growing, CEOs—even of NGOs—are under pressure from their boards to grow faster.'

Henry opened his iPad, 'Let me read to you a recent article about this problem. Here it is: A powerful charity's poisonous culture.[7] The charity it is talking about is the Silicon Valley Community Foundation. It is supported by Silicon Valley technology executives who have amassed enormous fortunes in recent years. It manages assets worth some $13.5 billion, making it larger than the Ford Foundation and the Rockefeller Foundation. Only the Bill and Melinda Gates Foundation and the Open Society Foundations are larger. The article says:

'Inside the Silicon Valley Community Foundation, which counts "inclusiveness", "integrity" and "respect" among its core values, a toxic culture festered for years, recently setting off a crisis that has now claimed three top executives.' It also says that this toxic culture was caused by the drive to scale up and become bigger.

'There was this bigger is better mentality,' said Dory Gannes, who worked in the foundation for two years, quitting it in 2016 after what she said was a dispute with Ms Loijens (the charity's chief fund-raiser, who was compelled to resign when the scandals

---

[7] NY Times International Edition, 14 May 14, 2018

surfaced). 'Our world was driven by scale—how many clients we had, how many grants we processed, how many countries we made grants to.'

Shape and structures of systems

Nancy was intrigued with Henry's comment on sizes and shapes of systems. In fact, the essence of systems thinking, as she had understood so far, was appreciation for the underlying structures that create a system. These structures are the forces that, by their presence and their interactions with each other, give the system its properties. They are like the flows in the cardiovascular system, the digestive system and the nervous system that enable the human body to function, or in the case of complex socio-economic systems, these could be flows in the economic system, social systems and the political system, that interact with each other and shape the whole system. Such structures are not visible to the eye. However, by observing a system from many angles, they can become visible, like an MRI can reveal the hidden structures within the human body. The reason we cannot understand the forces within complex systems easily, Senge says, is that causes and effects within them may be separated widely, both in time and space.

The changing shapes of populations is an example of cause and effect separated by a long time. Control on the population, which China and Singapore exercised very well decades ago, has now created economic and social problems for which they must find solutions. Perhaps they could have predicted that if they reduced the numbers of births and children, there would be fewer persons to produce babies in the future. Demographic scientists study the quantifiable growth, density and changing shapes of populations. Surely, they would have projected that the shape of the population would change. However, they may not have foreseen the impact the changing shape of the population would have on the conditions of the countries' economies and societies, the study of which falls within the domains of other scientific disciplines.

Having fewer children and controlling the population benefitted countries' economies. Per capita incomes were higher with fewer people, and there were less people to provide public services to. But what governments did not foresee so easily were the second-order effects on their societies of economic growth and fewer children. Family patterns changed. Women went to work. They married later. They had less desire to have babies than their mothers and grandmothers had. Now these governments want women to produce more babies. But the shape of the complex socio-economic system has changed too much meanwhile. It is difficult to change the shape of the system now to restore the balance between young and old persons in the population. The effect of controlling population on social norms is an example of causes and effects that fall in the purviews of different scientific disciplines. Specialists in demographics and other social studies operate largely within their own silos. They are mentally separated from each other.

Another example of causes and effects lying in different domains is the inter-connection between economic growth and environmental degradation. Economists wishing to increase GDP and economic growth have been ignoring the impacts of economic growth on the environment. Now, they are becoming concerned that the deterioration of the environment and climate change will have negative effects on economic growth. When causes and effects lie in different scientific silos, solutions by experts to problems in one part of the system can have unintended consequences. They can become problems for other parts of the system. Short-term fixes may succeed with unintended consequences that emerge later. The diagram illustrates the consequences of successful economic (and population control) policies that countries are now facing because the shapes of their populations have changed.

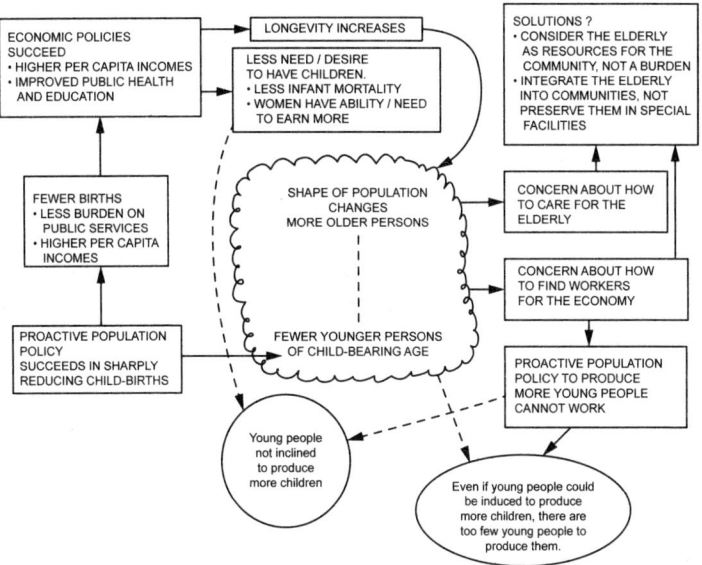

Fig 3. Examples of Fixes That Produce Unintended Consequences After Long Time-delays

In his book, Senge describes 'balancing loops' within systems. He explains how, when one part of a system grows too fast, out of sync with other forces, the system takes corrective action. A simple example is a system of rabbits and foxes. Foxes eat rabbits. However, if they eat too many and the population of rabbits declines, the foxes will not have enough food. Then the population of foxes will decline. If the population of foxes declines too much and rabbits begin to overrun the earth, the rabbits may eat up all the roots and vegetation around them. Then, they will begin to die of hunger and their population will reduce. Thus, foxes, rabbits and the vegetation around them are an integrated system. The lesson is, whatever your goal be, always keep the health of the whole system in mind, otherwise you will suffer.

Henry said, 'I like your explanation of causes and effects separated in time and in space. I think the corporate sector has become too short-term oriented and too narrowly focused.

"Execute. Implement. Stay focused. Act fast" are the mantras. The focus on quarterly results and the attention to daily gyrations of stock prices motivates actions to produce short-term results. The consequences in the future of these actions is of less interest to CEOs whose performances seem to be under scrutiny every quarter, or even sooner, by stock markets, and whose rewards are tied to stock prices. Staying focused on the growth of revenues and the bottom line leaves little room for concerns about longer-term impacts on the environment, and on society, of their corporations' short-term successes. Those effects are "externalities" that do not seem to fit into the prevalent corporate calculus.'

While Henry was speaking, Nancy was noting what he was saying. She was also listening to him—the person speaking, not just the words. He was a very committed young man. A young man with a young family, not just her boss. She put her notebook down and asked Henry, 'There is a question I have wanted to ask you. We never seem to get time together to reflect. May I ask you this question now?'

When Nancy asked Henry if she could ask him a question, he was intrigued by the look in her eyes. This was not going to be an ordinary question. He wondered what was on her mind. What could the question be?

'Yes, please ask,' he said to Nancy. 'Let us get something to drink first. It is becoming quite warm here. I am going to have a beer. What about you?'

'A lemonade,' Nancy said.

Henry walked over to the poolside bar and bought their drinks.

- Structures of forces acting together give a system its shape.
- A system's shape matters more for its health than does its size.
- When causes and effects are separated widely by space or time, it is not easy to foresee the unintended consequences of fixes to one part of the system. The fixes can backfire in another part of the system, and appear much later too.

11

Local Solutions to Global Problems

'What's the question, Nancy?' Henry asked.

'Are you enjoying your work, Henry? It must be very hard to keep our organization going, with the great difficulties we are facing while raising enough financial resources. Alongside that, you have to convert our organization from a conventional international NGO into something else—a network. It must be very difficult to "redesign the airplane while flying"—our board chair's favourite metaphor.'

'Actually, I am enjoying my work immensely,' Henry said. 'We are creating something new. It is always exciting to create something new—to bring about an innovation. It is exhilarating to be part of a "start-up". Innovations can happen, not only in technology; though, with all the hype about technology, it would appear that, if you are innovative, you must be doing something with technology. However, innovations can take place in creating new shapes of organizations and new systems of governance, which can produce great benefits for societies just as new technologies can. What we are working on is the shaping of an innovative, networked form of organization. It is exciting, but risky too, to redesign an airplane while flying.'

'What I am finding most rewarding personally is that I am learning a lot,' Henry continued. 'I studied Economics at Oxford. My learning agenda has broadened considerably since we have embarked on the redesigning of our airplane. I am reading about shifting paradigms in the sciences—the emergence of a new economics, the questions that development economists are now asking themselves about why their theories have not worked well to produce results in many countries. And, of course, I am reading whatever I can about shaping networked organizations. Our chair is a good coach for me. Though he is in India, we talk every month or so. I share what is on my mind with him. And he points me to ideas that might be useful, and to books and articles to read.'

'What is the secret stuff you keep noting down in that little black book?' Nancy asked Henry. 'Would you share it?'

'Sure,' Henry said, and opened his notebook. 'Whenever something strikes me as interesting—a question, a quotation, or a thought—I note it down. Much of it may not make sense to anyone else. For example, here I have written, and please don't laugh, "Humpty Dumpty fell off the wall with the European Enlightenment. Now all the king's horses and all the king's men must put Humpty Dumpty together again." The comment is not as weird as it may sound. It is much related to what you said about causes and effects being separated into different silos of scientific disciplines. Since the sixteenth century, the European Enlightenment has propagated scientific approaches to learning. The scientific approach is—first, look at the facts. Then, generate plausible explanations. Thereafter, test the hypothesis empirically. Accept as true only that which can be scientifically proven with data. This rational, scientific temper has enabled huge progress in many fields.

'As the scope of sciences expanded, the sciences began to break out into narrower specializations. Experts began to know more and more about only their parts of the system. Thus, knowledge of the whole system was broken apart into pieces. Each new branch or sub-branch of the sciences developed its own jargon, and its own priesthood. The parts could not understand each other. That is how systems thinking fell apart. Now, we are trying to put Humpty Dumpty together again with systems thinking. To create a new enlightenment.

'Here is another note: "Trying to 'manage' socio-economic development is like applying a non-systems approach to a systems problem." We were talking about this before I went to buy our drinks. Good management, the way it is generally understood and the way it is taught in management schools, says you must focus, measure and weed out whatever is not contributing to the concrete results you want. Also, you must produce results faster. Such principles of good management are overtaking the development sector too. Funders want objectives and plans to be made clear in measurable terms and progress to be periodically reported in the same measurable terms. This approach produces efficiency, no doubt. But it narrows down managers' attention to the immediate and it puts blinkers on their eyes. They do not see the full picture. Most big, development challenges, such as those listed in the SDGs, are systems challenges. A systems orientation is necessary to make improvements. Fixing only one part very efficiently, with prevalent good management practices, may harm other parts of the system.'

'There is a systems thinking term for it,' Nancy interjected. 'Such non-systemic interventions are called "fixes that backfire". In fact, the drive to increase GDP, mindless of its effects on the environment and inequality, is an example of a big fix that seems to be backfiring.'

'I studied Economics in Oxford, as I said,' Henry continued. 'Robert Lucas, who received the Nobel Prize in Economics for expounding the "rational expectations" view of human behaviour, referred to a theory as something that can be put on a computer and run. Many economists insist on equations and numbers because that is all that computers can compute. Economists' computations are focused on quantities. They strip out unquantifiable qualities from their pictures of reality. Lately, some economists have begun to question their own profession. They say that economists' desires to quantify, measure and compute—perhaps to appear more rigorous and scientific, like physicists—is making them miss the shape of the woods while they are counting the trees. Hardly any economist could predict the financial crisis, even though economists had reams of numbers about all major economies. One or two economists, like Raghuram Rajan (who later became the governor of India's Reserve Bank), who said a crisis was brewing, were dismissed as mavericks by the mainstream.

'Now economists seem to be expanding the scope of their models. They admit that human beings are not rational machines, and they also have emotions which influence their economic decisions. Economists are beginning to internalize forces, which they have so far treated as externalities in their models of reality. They are beginning to broaden their view of the system. However, if they insist on quantification and computation, they will not be able to fit qualitative forces into the same picture.'

'Systems thinking methods will help them make more complete models,' Nancy said. 'From what I have read so far, systems thinkers insist that all critical forces, whether or not they can be quantified, must appear in the picture of the system. The objective is to understand the relationships amongst the forces, not their sizes. Systems thinking methods privilege the production of visual maps of systems, rather than equations—visualization rather than calculation. The advantage of making pictures is that different sorts of things can be included in them. Pictures also enable easier communication amongst people who may not speak the same language. Thus, inputs about conditions in the system can be taken from diverse people, and the system can be seen from many perspectives. Each person can see only a part of the system. By including all parts, the whole system can be seen. It is like the fabled story of the blindfolded men around the elephant, each able to feel only one part. The one touching the tail thinks he has a rope in his hand. Another touching the trunk thinks it is a tree. Only when the views of all the blindfolded men are combined are all of them able to know they are touching a huge elephant!'

'You said you had some notes about networked organizations. Will you share them?' Nancy asked Henry. 'As you know, I am responsible for building the network.'

'Ah yes!' Henry said. 'In fact, this book I am reading, which our chair recommended to me, is about building a networked organization. It is the story of the creation of the global Visa credit-card network, written by its founder, Dee Hock.'

Nancy looked at the cover. The title was *One from Many: Visa and the Rise of Chaordic Organization*.[8] Peter Senge, whose book on systems thinking she was reading, had written the Foreword to the book.

'I have not yet read the whole book,' Henry explained. 'However, I have already found parts of it promising. Visa is an organization that is present everywhere. Members of its network include millions of merchants and thousands of banks in almost every country of the world. It works seamlessly without anyone controlling their transactions with each other. Visa has a small central node and other nodes distributed in the network. The huge, globe-spanning network was formed by several networks in different parts of the world coalescing voluntarily.'

'Wow! Sounds like the network we want to create,' Nancy said.

'It does,' agreed Henry. 'And let me read you some bits from the book. They will remind you about our discussions in the board meeting yesterday about the governance of our network and the need for a process to discover shared values amongst its members. Senge says in the foreword that what Dee Hock accomplished was "the organization of a network with no central authority". A network of free agents, none of whom understand the whole of the network nor do they need to, but each of whom knows the ground rules for participating.

Dee Hock says that in between chaos and order is a fluid, yet orderly state, which is neither chaotic nor controlled by anyone. When a system is in this state, creativity happens and innovations emerge. He uses Nature as an example of such a 'chaordic' system. Many systems within Nature interact with each other and co-evolve. None is superior to the other. All need each other. Nature

---

[8]Berret-Koehler Publishers, 2005.

is always evolving and adapting, though there is no one visibly in charge of its evolution.'

Henry turned to a page he had flagged. Here, Dee Hock said, 'The essential thing to remember is not that we became a world of expert managers and specialists, but the nature of our expertise became the creation of uniformity and efficiency, while the need has become the understanding and coordination of variability and complexity, the very process of change itself.'

And on another page, he said, 'The centre (the bank) should be the leader of a movement, not the commander of a structure.'

'So much unlearning to do!' Henry said. 'We will have to unlearn many prevalent ideas of management and organization embedded in our minds to make room for new ideas that will enable us to create the global network we want to form for the care of the elderly—a network in which we will be only a small, catalytic node, not the boss.'

'You remind me of some notes I made on the way back from the visit to the IGSHG that I wanted to discuss with you,' Nancy said to Henry. 'Each of these hundreds of groups of the elderly forming across Vietnam and in neighbouring countries is a centre for action for the care of the elderly. They learn to organize their meetings, make plans and to use their resources, which is mostly their own time, to take care of elderly persons who need assistance in their community. They visit those who are lonely and they assist those who need help with household chores, or who have medical needs. They also enrol younger people as volunteers in their groups. The younger people are able to perform functions in the groups that older people often cannot. Thus, the generations work together to improve the care of people in their communities—mostly elderly persons, but others too who may be in great need.

'What our board members were discussing on the long bus-ride to the hotel was the role that the elderly persons were playing in their communities. They had taken charge of their own care, cooperatively. They did not appear as supplicants of assistance from others. Instead, they had become a resource for the improvement of the community. This is the shift we, as a global network, want to bring about in the minds of not just older persons, but policymakers as well, that the elderly, whose numbers will keep increasing, are the world's fastest-growing, and so far the least used resource mankind has. Our board members said that what they saw in the IGSHGs was turning the notion of development assistance on its head. Target groups for assistance, such as the elderly, can and must be active agents of change, not merely passive beneficiaries. Networks must form in which assistance is not trickling down from some benign, distant centre. Rather, change must happen on the ground led by people who know what they need, muster their own resources and pull in the support they need from others, as they are doing from our local network partners in Vietnam.

'Two of the board members were with us at the international board meeting in Dar-E-Salaam, and had visited the older persons' associations (OPA) our network partners in Tanzania are supporting. They commented on the similarities and differences between the groups in Vietnam and Tanzania. The similarity was in the fundamental concepts, of enabling older persons to take charge, providing them with some training in how to organize themselves, coaching them as they go along and in nudging government agencies and philanthropies with resources to connect with and support these groups. The differences were in their agendas and the formats of their meetings. The problems and the resources available were different in the two countries. The formats of their meetings reflected cultural differences. Nevertheless, both were good examples of bottom-up solutions to the global problem of providing better care for the elderly. So, here is the note I made: "Local solutions to global problems. Not global solutions to local problems." A global network, like ours, addressing a global issue must encourage and enable more local solutions, instead of imposing a standard global solution top-down, which seems to be the underlying paradigm for most global programmes. Such solutions cannot fit all local contexts. Moreover, they make people dependent on those above, rather than empowering them.'

'Seems to me that this is how Nature works,' said Henry. 'It finds locally appropriate solutions to global problems of sustainability. There is an implication in what you have said—local solutions to global problems. The meta global problem is a breakdown in systems due to lack of systems thinking. "Humpty Dumpty falling apart!" Local solutions are required but they must be systemic too. Local agents of change, such as the IGSHGs, must learn to apply systems thinking more systematically to the challenges in their local environments. They must always consider the impacts of their actions on all parts of the local system. For example, solutions to improve livelihoods must improve the condition of the natural environment too. We should introduce systems thinking methods into the agendas of the IGSHGs and the OPAs. We must learn to apply systems in our own work too.'

- The problem is we are applying 'non-systems' (siloed) approaches to solve 'systems' problems.
- We need more local systemic solutions to solve global systemic problems.

12

Unlearning and Rethinking

Priya was deeply committed to her work with the Pune Community Welfare Sanstha. It fulfilled a deep desire to improve the lives of less privileged people. She did not consider what she did as charity work. She was not just handing out food, clothing or money for education and medical expenses to poor people in need. She was helping them to learn and earn and take charge of their surroundings. The outcome of the sanstha's work was not merely better-fed and better-clothed people. The result was people with more confidence in themselves and more dignity in their lives.

The purpose of the sanstha's work and the reason for its existence, stated in the poster framed in its CEO Usha Gore's office, was to, 'enable even the poorest amongst us to confidently stand on their own feet with dignity'. The deepest satisfaction Priya found in her work was not merely from the improvement in the living conditions of people in the communities in which the sanstha worked. It was from the change in the spirits of the people—the heads held high and the self-confidence expressed in their eyes.

It is not easy to measure self-confidence and dignity. Therefore, it was very difficult to satisfy donors' requirements to state the outcomes of the sanstha's work in measurable terms. It was much easier to state the numbers of women who would be trained in useful trades, how many children would be immunized, and how many cooking stoves would be converted from wood or coal to gas, etc. And so, such measurements could be obtained for the donors and the progress reported accordingly.

Priya knew many NGOs faced the challenge of converting the purpose of their work into the measurement frameworks of fund-providers. She wanted to learn how they were handling it. She heard about a forum, the Aspire Forum, in which NGOs and fund-providers were meeting to learn together on how they could cooperate more effectively to produce better outcomes on larger scales. The Forum's participants met for three-day retreats twice a year. She received an invitation to their next retreat, which would be in an ashram not far from Pune.

Priya asked the sanstha's CEO, Usha Gore, for permission to take some time off for the retreat. Usha was pleased that Priya was so interested to learn more about the ways in which the social sector worked. The sanstha was very fortunate to have someone with Priya's talents to help with the relationship building and fund-raising from philanthropic foundations and corporations, which were essential for the sanstha's work, but which Usha found very difficult.

Usha had studied at the Tata Institute of Social Sciences (TISS) decades ago. She had done fieldwork in the slums of Mumbai. She had learned about the human and social sides of communities, and excelled in that area. Priya, on the other hand, was a graduate of one of India's best institutes of business management. She had been a brilliant student. She could talk in the jargon of management, money and measurement with providers of funds whenever it was necessary. Usha could not. Usha also knew that Priya had made a great financial sacrifice to work with the sanstha. She could have joined a consulting firm or a large MNC and earned a very big salary, just like her classmates. Hence, Usha wanted to make sure that Priya found her work satisfying. It pleased her to see Priya absorbed in in the sanstha's mission and she was more than willing to give Priya the days off she was asking for to participate in the retreat. It was the least Usha could do for her.

Priya had been sponsored to the Forum by Nishant, who described himself as a 'social entrepreneur'. He was in his fifties. He was a very senior alumnus of the same management institution Priya had been to. Nishant had joined a technology company in India briefly and moved to Silicon Valley with a start-up, which was doing very well. When the start-up was sold to a larger company, its founders and Nishant made a lot of money. He invested in other start-ups and they succeeded as well. When he was in his forties, Nishant had made more money than he could have imagined he would when he had graduated from his management institute in India twenty years ago.

Then, he came to a big turn in the road when a midlife crisis hit him. What would he do with the rest of his life? He had made more than enough money. It was less than his neighbours, but much more than what he needed. His large home, in a small town south of San Francisco, had more bedrooms and bathrooms than his wife and he needed, and a swimming pool as well. Some of his neighbours' homes were mansions even bigger than his. His wife and he drove luxury cars. At the same time, some of his neighbours seemed to have stables of expensive cars; sedans, sports cars and SUVs—a car for every occasion.

Sometimes, when conversations turned to who had what, which they often did in the 'go-go' culture of Silicon Valley, he did feel an urge to catch up with them. However, whenever he talked to his parents back in India, he would realize again, how far he had come in life. He had grown up in an upper middle-class Indian family. His father was a senior official in the government, much respected in the community. They had a decent home and one car. They were very comfortable compared to most of the people around them, especially the masses of poor people who one could not ignore in India. Nishant realized, in his midlife crisis, what he cared about most deeply. It was an urge to make the world better for the most deprived people, and he cared about it more than making himself more successful and wealthier. He felt the time had come to 'give back'. His son—his only child—had graduated from a good college in the US and already had a well-paying job with a rising technology company in the Valley. His wife was concerned about her ageing parents back in India, and about Nishant's parents too. Their son could look after himself. She was happy to return to India with Nishant.

After returning to India, Nishant looked for opportunities to invest in enterprises whose mission was to serve the 'bottom of the pyramid'. There was so much to be done—to provide better sanitation, clean energy, better housing, better healthcare, and better education to millions of people in India. India's shining GDP numbers—sometimes touted as the fastest-growing free market democracy in the world (to distinguish it from authoritarian China which was growing faster)—camouflaged many deprivations and injustices that hundreds of millions of its citizens suffered from.

The problem was huge and complicated. How could he make a difference? It seemed to him that he could start with finding people already engaged with the system who had already found some ways to make a difference. Most likely, such people would need more financial resources to scale up their initiatives. He could offer them some money to assist them. And, if they would let him engage with them in their work, he could learn more about the challenges of economic development and social change.

Nishant discovered that he was not alone in this quest. There were other 'social entrepreneurs' like him searching for better models of development. With some of them, he conceived the idea of the Aspire Forum, a forum in which they could interact with social organizations in India and learn together how they could cooperatively change the prevalent system to improve the lives of poorer people faster and on a larger scale. The founders of the Forum pooled some money to pay for the accommodations and facilities required for their meetings. These meetings were held in simple places, such as hostels and ashrams, which provided clean and inexpensive accommodations. They were economical, and they also seemed more appropriate than five-star hotels to discuss how poverty could be reduced.

Nishant was on the lookout for people to invite to the Forum's meetings, who would contribute to the group's collective learning, such as heads of NGOs and CEOs of philanthropic foundations. Lately, he had begun to look out for younger people who had volunteered to work in social change. They would be the leaders of change in the future. They could benefit from the discussions in the Forum. That is how he had found Priya, whose name had been recommended to him by a common friend of Usha Gore's and his.

Priya was delighted to be included in the Forum's meeting. In the group were leaders of many NGOs she admired, as well as officers of philanthropic foundations and development agencies she would have loved to have more contact with to raise support for her sanstha. The meeting began with a round of 'checking in'. In turn, everyone spoke about what had brought them to the Forum, what were some big questions on their minds, and what they were hoping to learn during the meeting. When Priya's turn came, she humbly thanked everyone for including her in the meeting. She said that she had come to learn from people whom she admired very much. When she was prodded to say what was on her mind, she said she wondered how, with so many devoted people each doing great work, the pace of poverty removal was so slow. Were more devoted people needed or could there be another, fundamentally different, and more effective way? Priya quoted a statement often attributed to Albert Einstein: 'You cannot solve the difficult problems before you with the same approach that has caused the problems.'

Nishant explained the agenda of the meeting. It included talks by two guests. One was a greatly respected leader of the social sector in India, who had built a large organization well known for its work in poverty removal. The other was a thought leader who has been thinking and writing about systems change.

Priya was looking forward to listening to both of them, especially to the 'systems thinker'. In her 'learning notebook', her constant companion, she had written down several questions about structures of systems and how systems change. She hoped to fill her notebook with many ideas. She was not disappointed.

> We are unlikely to produce results faster by putting more resources into the same approaches that have caused the problems we are facing.

13

Three Models of Systems

The systems teacher startled the Forum with this opening question: 'You want to change the world. Has the world given you permission to change it?'

The eager change-makers were taken aback.

'Why do you want to change the world?' he asked.

'Because we can,' they responded.

'Caring for your patient is essential for you to be a good doctor,' the teacher said, 'but not sufficient. You must know how to help the patient too.'

Three models

He said, 'To know how you can help any complex system become better, whether it is the human body or a social system, you must have three models in your mind: 'First of all, you must have a good model of the system itself. A doctor wishing to improve a patient's health must have a good model of what goes on inside the body. What are the various organs, how do they interact with each other. Would you trust a doctor who does not know how your body's systems work to operate on you? Not knowing what is inside and where, a surgeon could even kill the patient while trying to make her better. A specialist who prescribes a strong medicine to heal the digestive system must know the side effects the medicine may have on the cardiac system, and vice versa. Otherwise, the patient may die of the side effects of a well-intended treatment by a doctor who does not know how the whole system functions. If you want the body to get well enough to not need more medical interventions, you must also understand how the body heals itself, because what you must do while treating the disease in the body is to also restore the body's own healing capacities.

'Therefore, the second model a good doctor must have is the model of the body's internal healing systems. A good doctor must understand what gives a body the strength to recover and repair itself and he must assist these internal forces to become stronger. With these two models in mind, the doctor can develop the third model, which is the model of practice—of how a doctor should assist the internal systems of the body to heal and strengthen themselves.'

The three models provided a simple and logical framework.

Two scientific laws

The teacher then asked how many of the participants had studied engineering or science. A few hands went up.

The teacher asked, 'Can you tell the others what the Second Law of Thermodynamics is?

One of the students answered, 'The Second Law of Thermodynamics says that the internal entropy of a system must inevitably increase with time.'

'Correct,' said the teacher. 'The Second Law of Thermodynamics, which every engineer knows and must respect, is that disorder within a system will increase over time and its useful energy will dissipate. Therefore, over time, the capability of a machine will decrease. An old automobile will not have the same pep as a new one.'

The teacher drew a chart on the board. Against the vertical axis, he wrote, 'Internal Order/Capability.' Along the horizontal axis, he wrote, 'Time.' He drew a diagonal line from the top left corner to the bottom right-hand corner. 'This line represents the

Second Law of Thermodynamics,' he said, 'which says that the capabilities of all machines will reduce over time.'

Then he drew another diagonal line from the bottom left corner to the top right corner of the chart. He added, 'Here is another fundamental law of science. This is the law of evolution. It says that complex systems acquire higher order capabilities over time. From amoebae to insects and reptiles, and onto mammals, apes and humans, Nature has moved for millennia along this trajectory. Humans have higher order capabilities, which earlier species did not have.'

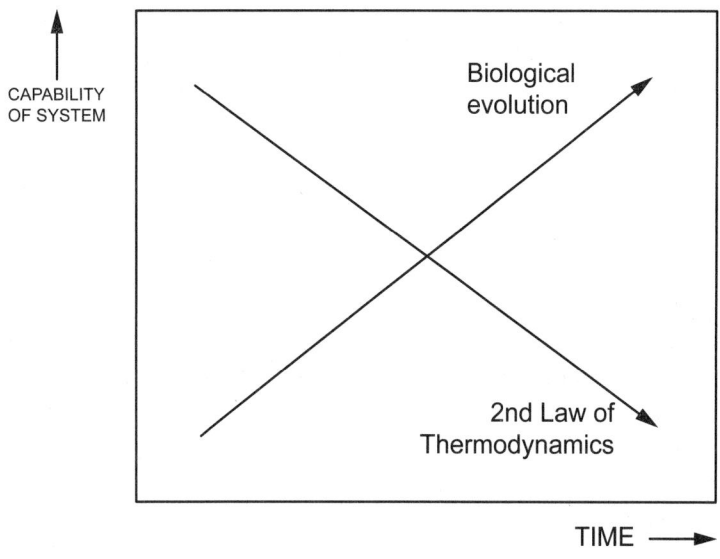

Fig 4. Two Scientific Laws

He continued, 'We have observed the law of evolution in operation, and we have also observed the Second Law of Thermodynamics in operation. They seem to be in contradiction with each other. So, which is true?'

The participants were perplexed.

'Both are true,' the teacher said. 'Each in its own domain.

Let me ask the engineers if anyone can explain this conundrum.'

One of them hesitatingly said, 'Maybe the explanation is that the Second Law says that in a closed system the entropy will increase.'

'You are right,' the teacher said. 'Mechanical systems are closed, or bounded systems, whereas systems in Nature are open systems. They have permeable boundaries. They take energy from each other and give energy to each other too. If you seal any part of Nature off from the rest, it cannot sustain itself. It will wither unless you can artificially nurture it forever. Engineering disciplines have enabled men to acquire great power over Nature. Massive dams have been built, rivers diverted, forests cleared, artificial materials produced, plants genetically engineered, and now human babies can be genetically engineered too.

'With the scientific mindset, that has spread around the world with the European Enlightenment since the seventeenth century, scientific man's relationship with Nature has become that of an observer outside Nature, objectively studying it, and acquiring more power to re-engineer it to serve his own purposes. Development experts try to look at societies objectively and scientifically. They design solutions to improve societies and then try to impose their expert solutions onto societies. Those societies that resist solutions that appear to them to be inappropriate are accused of being backward, of resisting modernization, and suffering from a "Not Invented Here" syndrome, whereas what they may be saying to the well-intentioned doctor is that their solution is causing them pain. They may be asking them to slow down, and first understand how their bodies work before prescribing medicines for them. Before you work on improving a complex system with the best of intentions, you must understand the structures of the system and its sources of energy to improve itself, just as a good doctor must before prescribing strong medicines. Therefore, let us understand what are the structures of systems that have an inherent ability to evolve and do not need to be externally engineered all the time.'

Three types of systems

The teacher continued, 'Broadly, complex systems may be divided into three classes of systems. One is "engineered" systems. These are systems designed by humans, following scientific disciplines, to produce desired outcomes. Machines are the most common manifestation of this class of systems, so are top-down planning systems that try to control inputs and outputs of organizations. However, as all students of engineering must learn, engineered systems are subject to the Second Law of Dynamics. The operation of the law is evident in our experience. Machines must be periodically repaired and renovated by engineers to maintain their levels of performance. And we also know from experience that while planned economies may start vigorously, they lose their abilities over time, as the Soviet economy did.

'The second class of systems is "chaotic" systems. These are formed by the interactions of millions of independent particles or free agents. The concept of a free market composed of free agents operating without any governmental regulation, that liberal market extremists espouse, has the structure of a chaotic system. Chaotic systems can produce surprising outcomes. The example of a butterfly flapping its wings in Brazil that causes storms in Hong Kong is often cited to illustrate this characteristic of chaotic systems. The near collapse of the global financial system, stemming from problems in the housing loan market in the USA, could be another example. Mathematicians and physical scientists are trying to understand the structures within chaotic systems that can propagate consequences of local events onto other distant parts of the system.

'However, it is the third class of systems that is of most interest to us. These are complex "self-adaptive" systems. Insights into these have come from a collaborative, interdisciplinary exploration of systems by economists, physical scientists, evolutionary biologists, computer systems experts and others interested in the behaviour of complex systems. One of the best known interdisciplinary forums is the Santa Fe Institute. It was founded in 1984 in Santa Fe, USA, by Nobel laureates in economics and the physical sciences and eminent theoretical biologists and computer scientists.

'Complex self-adaptive systems display characteristics that neither engineered systems nor chaotic systems have. They increase their capabilities over time unlike engineered systems, and they do this with some underlying logic, unlike random chaotic systems. The most obvious illustrations of such systems are in Nature where capabilities of species evolve through competition. Thus, over time, more evolved species develop. Contrary to the Second Law of Thermodynamics, natural systems follow a law of evolutionary biology that says that complex systems will increase their capability over time. Competition in Nature does not destroy the whole system. There is some higher order, or some deeper structures—depending on whether one believes in God or is an atheist—that regulates this competition so that the 'commons' on which all depend are maintained. On these commons, the competitive game plays out, evolving better capabilities in the system over time. Complex self-adaptive systems sit "on the edge" between engineered systems and chaotic systems. They neither sink into stasis like engineered systems nor are they an unformed, potentially chaotic mess. They have an underlying architecture that gives them the capability to evolve from lesser order to higher order. People like us, with a passion to help societies improve themselves, must understand the principles that give complex systems self-adaptive capabilities.

Architectural principles

'The question is: What can we learn from the emerging research into complex self-adaptive systems such as biological systems that would apply to the design of human institutions and organizations? To answer this question, a framework that describes the essential elements of an organized human system is necessary. We need this filter or lens through which we can select what is applicable from the fascinating material that is becoming available on complex self-adaptive systems. Without the filter, one could pick up a bunch of curious and romantic ideas that may not be applicable human institutions. At the same time, the filter must be broad enough so that it does not screen out any unusual idea, merely because it does not fit the detailed mental model of the filter designer about what is relevant to business and social organizations.

'An organized human system (a definition that covers business entities, government organizations, and NGOs) consists of four fundamental components. Firstly, all such systems use "resources" of many types. These include people, technologies, machines, etc. The composition of resources varies with the nature of the entity. Secondly, these resources are "organized" in some manner. Thirdly, the resources in the enterprise are deployed in "processes" to produce results. Last but not least, all these—the processes, organization, and resources—must be directed towards the purpose of the enterprise. So, purpose, organization processes and resources are the four fundamental components. These four seem to be the minimum set of components required to describe a social or business system. Take any one of them away and the description seems incomplete. More can be added but they would most likely be an expansion of one of these four basic building blocks.

'The study of complex self-adaptive systems reveals one critical principle for each of the four components of a complex human system, thereby making a minimal critical set of principles. The systems teacher drew a sketch on the whiteboard. He explained each principle with a few bullet points.'

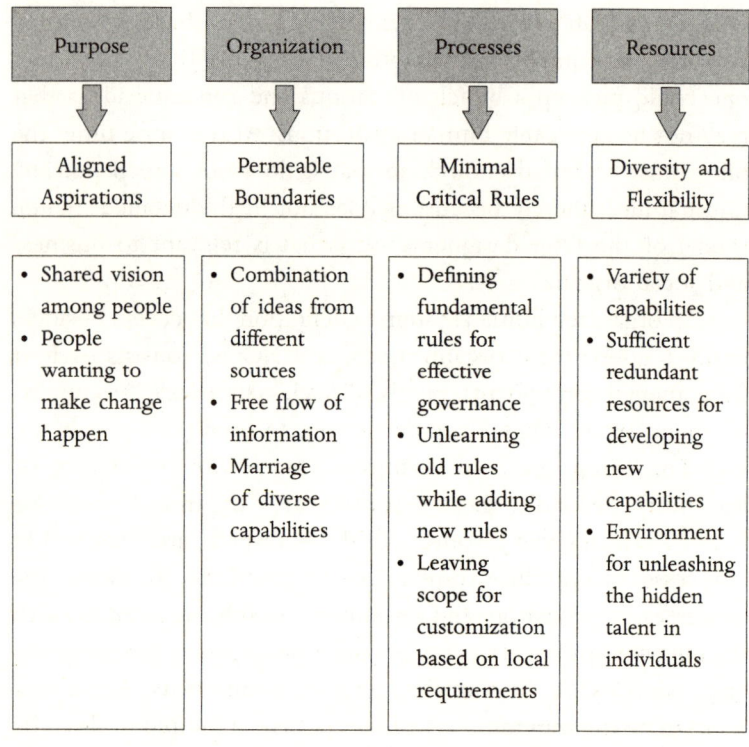

Fig 5. The Architectural Principles of Complex Self-adaptive Systems

Aligned aspiration

'Human systems differ from all other, non-human, complex systems with regard to the process of choosing goals and setting direction. Human beings have the ability and the urge to consciously project themselves into the future. They can visualize the futures they want to create and live in, whereas, as far as we know, other complex systems, such as ecological systems, do not have this ability. Perhaps these systems are also evolving towards some goal. But it is not clear whether the components of the system—the flora and fauna and the rest—have chosen the goal! Hence, there may not be much to be learned from complex self-adaptive systems which are not human, that may be relevant to the process by which human systems imagine their futures and set their goals.

'The principle that applies to the setting of direction in human organizations, ranging from business organizations and NGOs to nations, is "Aligned Aspirations". Both words are important. The goal has to be aspirational. It must be something people really care about and want, otherwise they will not be inspired to stretch themselves to create that future. And there has to be conscious alignment of aspirations and goals to get the force of many intelligences working together that can make seemingly impossible things possible.'

Permeable boundaries

The systems teacher further said, 'I will introduce the principles that apply to the other components by analyzing a complex self-adaptive system that is very modern and very "techie", and then support these principles by insights from natural systems. Let us consider the evolution of the Internet. The Internet is a very complex system in many ways. It connects many sub-systems all over the world, each of which works to its own rules. People are putting in and taking out things from the Internet all the time. It is also a very adaptive system. It enables functions that people have not conceived before. Innovations continue.

The power of the Internet comes from its ability to enable "end-to-end" connections. Switch the computer on. Write a message to anyone anywhere. Put the address. Click. And off it goes across boundaries of organizations and countries. It is widely acknowledged that the Internet has stimulated many innovations and social change by bringing a huge variety of ideas and people together very quickly and easily. There does not seem to be any significant field of human endeavour that has not already been touched by the Internet's innovative environment—business, education, research, government and entertainment too.

'Some people do not like that there should be so much

freedom. They have political, cultural, economic or technical reasons to wish to curtail this complete freedom, which they fear can lead to chaos. People in power rightly fear the consequences of this free flow of information and opinions to their constituents from all sorts of sources over the Internet. Hence, they try sometimes, like King Canute, to roll back the waves that may wash them away.

'Parents fear that their children may see and hear things they are not supposed to, as they surf the Internet. Napster stretched, beyond the limit perhaps, some current foundational principles of economics. By enabling Internet users to download free music, it violated the rights of the owners of intellectual property to obtain financial rewards for their creativity and investments.

'Shutting down boundaries between users will diminish the power of the Internet. On the other hand, it is becoming clear that some form of boundary control is necessary, otherwise social media will create political and social chaos. How to make social media boundaries adequately permeable is the social and technological challenge that the Internet giants and governments of countries are grappling with.

'In nature, life exists where boundaries meet and there is flow across them. The water's edge, where land and water mingle, is always the most fecund source of new forms of life. In nature also, cross-breeding is the source of healthy evolution, whereas in-breeding results in regression over time.

'There seems to be an inexorable tendency in organizations, in governments and in businesses, to create internal walls when they seek order and pursue efficiency. They create these walls within themselves by creating specialized roles, narrow performance evaluations and with incentive systems that reward individual contributions. All these measures—specialization, precise performance evaluations and incentives linked directly to individual and departmental performance—seem logical for managing an organization in a disciplined manner. But they very often result in reducing internal collaboration and creating internal silos. Therefore, leaders must continue to test whether there is permeability in the organization's boundaries.'

Minimal critical rules

The teacher continued, 'Let us now look at the third of the four components of organized, complex human systems, viz. processes. Let us get into this by asking the question, "What holds the Internet together?" The answer is a set of simple rules or protocols. The Internet and the World Wide Web have enabled people everywhere to communicate with each other and to send, search and store very complicated information on almost anything under the sun. Tim Berners-Lee, the inventor of the World Wide Web, has been hailed by *Time* magazine as one of the greatest minds of the twentieth century. In his book *Weaving the Web*, Mr Berners-Lee describes how the Web came about.[9] "The art was to define the few basic rules, common rules of protocol that would allow one computer to talk to another, in such a way that when all computers everywhere did it, the system would thrive, not break down. For the Web, those elements were, in decreasing order of importance, Universal Resource Identifiers (URIs), the Hypertext Transfer Protocol (HTTP), and the Hypertext Markup Language (HTML)."

'And Mr Berners-Lee adds, "What was often difficult for people to understand about the design was that there was nothing else beyond URIs, HTTP, and HTML. There was no central computer controlling the Web, no single protocol on which these protocols worked, not even an organization anywhere that ran the Web."

'Somehow, we have a mental model that anything huge, involving many people and lots of activity, must require a lot of effort to control it. We also believe that complex situations require complex solutions, whereas the truth is that complex situations are best resolved by very simple solutions and governed by very few rules. Chris Langton of the Santa Fe Institute has experimented with

---

[9]Tim Berners-Lee, 'Weaving the Web', *Harpers* San Francisco

the Game of Life, a computer programme that produces evolving "life-like" patterns. A few simple rules enable the programme to create very orderly patterns. When he added a few more rules to improve the patterns and to speed up the process, the system did not seem to respond well. If he added a few more rules to correct the side effects of the previous rules, the system started going into disorder. This intrigued Langton. All the rules were good rules. Each was added to take care of a problem that had been noticed. Then why did the system's performance deteriorate? It struck him that the number of rules, not just their goodness, has an effect on the system's capability to change and evolve gracefully.

'Stuart Kaufmann and John Holland have confirmed this. They experimented with computer programmes that learn new and better rules to be more effective. Holland developed the notion of an "economy of rules", which means that while a system needs rules to run itself, it needs only a minimal set of critical rules. So, the lesson is that while learning organizations will learn new rules, they must remember the principle of Minimal Critical Rules, and shed (unlearn) some rule as they add another good rule. Unfortunately, organizations are quick to add rules, and not at all systematic in shedding rules.'

Diversity and flexibility of resources

After a pause, the conversation continued: 'The fourth component in our framework of a complex human system is resources. Companies, communities and countries use resources to produce the value that they need. The resources include physical resources along with knowledge and talents of people. Organizations that wish to evolve to higher order capabilities must have flexibility in their resource pool. There are three ways in which organizations can ensure that they have the required flexibility in the resources available to them. One is by "requisite variety" in the resources. The second is through "adequate redundancy". A third way of obtaining flexibility is "latent potential" in the resources.

'Stephen Jay Gould, an authority on evolutionary biology, explains how these principles work in biological species, thereby enabling them to evolve. The principle of "requisite variety" is simplest to understand. Systems that do not have requisite variety run the danger of losing their vitality because of inbreeding. Hence, it is necessary to ensure that the gene pool is rich and sufficiently varied. One of the reasons why the USA is a source of many innovations in many fields is the variety of people that come together in the US "melting pot". It is worth noting that in the USA, immigrants are not restricted to the lower level, labour-intensive, jobs. They also occupy senior positions in corporations, academia and research, where they participate in shaping new ideas and policies. What this implies is that countries and companies that shut out outsiders from their knowledge-creating pools run the risk of stagnation. They may be very efficient while they lead in a game they have mastered. But when the game changes they are unable to innovate and change.

"Adequate redundancy" is perhaps the idea that efficiency-oriented managers have most difficulty with. But let us see why it is important. Consider the human body as an example. It is a very efficient machine. The chemical, physical and cognitive processes it can perform are amazing. These abilities are related to the genes in the body. We have now begun to understand how these genes work and what each one of them does. Let us suppose that every gene was required for a function of the human body and mind. In other words, a perfectly engineered or "re-engineered" machine, with all unnecessary genes removed. Now suppose the body needed to adapt itself to a new capability. Which gene could it spare to experiment and learn this capability? It could not afford to let any of its genes "off the hook" of what the gene was doing because that would affect the body's on-going functions. Hence, evolution of new capabilities would be severely hampered, if not impossible.

'The third way in which biological species have the capabilities in their resources to evolve is by "latent potential" in their resources.

Gould gives the example of birds developing wings to fly. Feathers are an essential component of a bird's flying apparatus. But birds did not originally develop feathers so that they could fly. Feathers were first developed for their thermal capabilities—to keep the bodies of birds warm. Later, the "latent potential" of feathers as flying apparatus was taken advantage of, when birds needed to fly to find food and to escape from predators. Imagine a "value engineer" examining a bird before birds had learned to fly. He would redesign the feathers to improve their thermal efficiency, or even replace them with something else even more effective for keeping the bird warm. Thus, he would unwittingly strip the feathers of their potential as flying apparatus. Thereby, he would create a very warm species of bird perhaps, but one that may soon die of hunger, or be gobbled up by a predator. A "value engineer", looking with a clinical eye at all parts of an organization, seeks to strip out the capabilities whose contribution to the performance of the system is not clear. Thus, latent capabilities that could be the source of valuable innovations can be thrown aside. We now have four principles, one for each of the four basic components of a complex human system. Let us recapitulate them:

- Purpose : Aligned Aspiration
- Organization : Permeable Boundaries
- Processes : Minimal Critical Rules
- Resources : Diversity and Flexibility

Four basic components; one fundamental principle for each.'

The participants in the Forum were fascinated by the simplicity and elegance of the framework. Only four components and four rules. It was internally self-consistent too, conforming to its own principle of minimal critical rules.

The systems teacher then asked, 'Any questions?' Someone asked, 'What about leadership? What skills do leaders need to lead within a complex self-adaptive system?'

Models of leadership

'I am very glad you asked,' the teacher said. 'Leadership models must be congruent with the architecture of the system in which leadership has to be exercised. You must recall the three models if you want to help a system improve itself. The first is to understand the structure of the system. The second is to understand how the system heals itself and grows. Then only can you figure out what you must do to help the system build its own capacity. Mechanical systems can be controlled by strong leaders who can tell all the parts what they must do and coordinate their actions. Such strong leaders sit atop their organizations, not within them. On the other hand, chaotic systems appear out of control. There is no alignment amongst the parts. Leadership, if there is any within them, is ineffectual. The relevant question for people working in the development space is: how should leadership be exercised within a complex self-adaptive system, and who should exercise it? This brings us back to the question I asked you at the very beginning. "You want to change the world. Has the world given you permission to change it?"

'For the system to be self-adaptive, the impetus for change and for taking charge of making change must be within the system. It must not be imposed from outside because then the system will remain dependent on an external engineer to make it do what it must. The entropy within the system will continue to increase. Well-meaning external donors and development workers will have to continue to inject time and resources to sustain the improvement. Whenever you want to help a community because you care and even when you are invited by the community to help them, you must be mindful of your own motivations and your own sources of satisfaction. Your motivation must be to enable the community to recover or discover its own ability to take charge.

'Moments of disengagement can be painful. The external leader gives so much of her time to help the community. She feels good whenever they ask for help, and she is able to give it. She has warm feelings when she is thanked. She feels wanted. Then, when she is no longer needed, she may miss the appreciations, and may even feel rejected by a community who had used her when they needed help.'

The teacher recalled the words of ancient Chinese wisdom. 'When a good king improved the lives of people in the kingdom, the people said he was a good king. When a great king improved the lives of the people, the people said we did it.'

1. Three models:
   - A model of what the system is
   - A model of how the system improves itself
   - A model of how one may help the system improve itself
2. Two scientific theories, seemingly in contradiction to each other
   - The Second Law of Thermodynamics, which applies to mechanical systems
   - The law of evolution, which applies to complex, self-adaptive, natural systems
3. Three types of systems
   - Engineered systems (closed systems)
   - Complex, self-adaptive systems (open systems)
   - Chaotic systems (unbounded systems)
4. Different leadership models for closed systems and open systems

14

Systems' Structures

In 2006, before the global financial crisis, when the Dow Jones was reaching new heights, an important meeting was convened in Cleveland. The subject of the meeting was 'Business as an Agent of World Benefit'. The provocation for the meeting was increasing evidence, from several multi-country surveys, of declining trust in business corporations. Evidently, even though, as consumers, people seemed satisfied with the products and services provided by corporations, and as investors, they seemed delighted by their stocks' performance, as citizens they expected much more of corporations.

The meeting was convened by the Academy of Management and the UN Global Compact. The Academy of Management is the largest organization of business management teachers in the world with more than 18,000 members. As one of its members said, it is the 'Teamsters Union' of business teachers. The UN Global Compact, founded in 2000, is an international organization of business corporations that volunteered to conduct their businesses in ways that would accelerate achievement of the Millennium Development Goals. Beginning with 40 members in 2000, the Compact had more than 3,000 members in six continents by 2006.

The backdrop of the meeting was the condition of people and the environment, neither of which seemed to be improving as rapidly as required to achieve the Millennium Development

Goals. Meanwhile, businesses were reporting sterling financial performance. Therefore, a lurking suspicion (contributing to the widespread mistrust of business corporations) was that not only are philanthropy and corporate social responsibility (CSR), which corporations do on the side, inadequate, but that the core operations of businesses may be, somehow, contributing to the unsatisfactory condition of people and the environment.

The meeting was attended by 450 persons from 40 countries—management students, business school teachers and administrators mostly, and corporate executives; another 1,000 people attended by webcast. Over three days, the meeting heard several thought leaders in the corporate and education worlds, discussed more than a hundred papers, and carried on a lively dialogue facilitated by David Cooperrider of Case Western University, using the principles of 'appreciative inquiry' that he has developed, whereby the intelligence of many participants can be combined in large meetings.

A round-table discussion with CEOs at the meeting focused on what business schools could do to help corporations deliver against their agenda of broader social responsibility. The contribution that the schools could make was divided into two parts—contribution through research about topics that business leaders considered important and the development of students with capabilities corporations would need.

Business and ethics

The research agenda suggested had two parts. One part was to establish the 'business case' by proving that corporations that deliver against the broader needs of society also produce better returns for their shareholders in the long run. Evidently, even though the CEOs present were personally motivated, they needed such evidence to justify their strategies to analysts and investors who take a more utilitarian view of corporate investments. The business case could cover the angle of future risks to corporations if they did not perform against society's broader expectations, as well as the improvement of the bottom line by reduced costs (by reducing energy consumption, etc.), and higher prices that could be obtained by building a more trusted corporate brand.

The second part of the research agenda was to develop the 'moral and ethical case' for doing good. Some CEOs felt that everything in business cannot and need not be justified in utilitarian terms. In fact, they felt that the view that unless something has a financial value it is not valuable has smothered concern for basic human needs. The morality discussion led to an intense debate about the schools' responsibilities for developing business graduates with good values.

Developing good managers

The CEOs, educators and students participating in the conference discussed the need to change the curriculum of management education. In the view of the CEOs, graduates produced by the management schools had a very narrow a view of the world. They were driven too much by the profit motive, in their own lives and in their view of business' role in society. The CEOs recommended that the management curriculum should be modified to include compulsory courses on the 'human condition' and the environment, and that the excessive emphasis on economics and finance should be reduced. Endorsing the need for a course correction, a respected American CEO went so far as to say that economics should be removed altogether because its fundamental assumptions about human behaviour were flawed and, instead, the students should be taught how to discover and relate to their conscience and the art of building human relationships!

The educators retorted that businesses are getting what they pay for and that students in the financial disciplines get the highest salaries. Therefore, in the spirit of putting one's money where one's mouth is, if businesses were to pay more to graduates in other disciplines, students would want to take those courses and the schools would offer them! However, the educators were in a bind. They admitted that the curriculum was too limited. They cited a study by Jeffrey Pfeffer of Stanford that showed that, whereas students broaden their thinking in other educational programmes, the MBA curriculum was the only educational programme that produced graduates who were narrower in their thinking when they left than when they entered the programme. The educators' problem was that business schools are rated by the salaries their students get after graduation and since students in the financial disciplines do get the highest salaries, schools must produce more of them to improve their ratings.

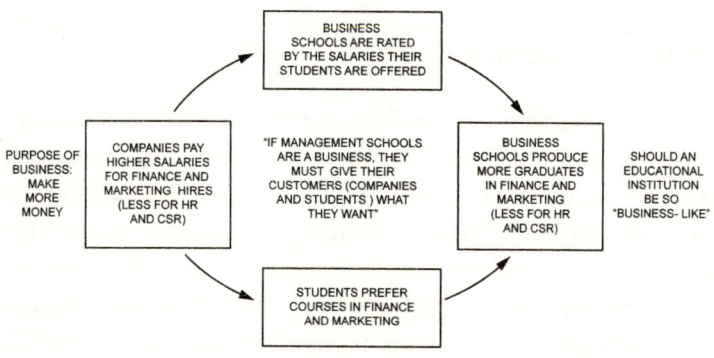

Fig 6. Companies, Business Schools and Students in a Reinforcing Loop: Who Will Begin the Change?

The views of the students themselves were revealing. A survey of 2,100 students in 87 business schools found that 87 per cent believed that corporations should work towards broader societal goals, but only 18 per cent believed corporations were doing so. Only 36 per cent felt business schools were preparing business managers to work for the betterment of society; 70 per cent wanted business schools to change their curriculum to develop socially and environmentally responsible individuals and 79 per cent said they wanted socially responsible jobs. What is also revealing is that while 63 per cent of the respondents said they would work for a medium and large company after graduation, only 33 per cent said they would continue to work there after five to ten years. Since they had to repay the loans, they had taken for their education, they needed the salaries the big companies paid, but after repaying the loans, they would rather do more socially responsible work.

The young teacher who presented the survey had selected two statements she thought expressed the students' feelings overall. One was: 'The key business role is to develop society, not profits.' The other: 'Profitability is easy: Changing the world is hard.'

Changing the world

Businesses, students and schools are part of a system, with each responding to the other. All of them wonder how the system can be changed so that business can play a more effective role as an 'agent for world benefit'. Who shall change first to begin the change in the system?

While discussing what would be required to make more corporations work for the greater good of society, the CEOs said that if their customers were to demand that companies act responsibly and if they were to buy only from those that do, businesses would change their behaviour very quickly. In other words, these CEOs are calling on customers to take the lead and pressurize business managers to change. They are saying that when people start acting like responsible citizens rather than as passive consumers, they can make the companies behave responsibly too.

The meeting highlighted that citizens, businesses, management schools and students are parts of a complex system. Donella Meadows, a doyen of systems thinking and the author of the report, *The Limits to Growth,* which pointed out in 1972 that the pattern of economic growth the world was following would lead to an environmental crisis, provided the insight that every system is perfectly designed to produce the results it is presently producing. All components of the system, responding to each other, are locked into a pattern, which is difficult to change. It is not clear who should take the lead to change the pattern when there is great risk that others will not follow.

Systems change requires leadership of a high, moral order. A leader in a system is he or she who takes the first steps towards what he or she deeply cares about, and in ways that others will wish to follow. A leader will take the first steps to create a path out of the inertia of the system. He or she does not wait for others for then he or she is not a leader. A leader will take the personal risks to step out of the comfort zone if he or she cares very deeply to produce an outcome that the locked-in system is not producing. Therefore, a leader must have a compelling case for change and also should communicate this case for change to others in terms they understand, and in which they can imagine how the world would become a better place for them.

Reorganizing or expanding a company, so that its share price increases and greater value is produced for shareholders, may motivate its CEO and other executives whose compensation will increase with the higher share price. But what value will the reorganization create for employees who will lose jobs, and what value will the expansion create for communities who fear the destruction of their environment? A higher 'GDP' may satisfy economists, but will it contribute to improvement of well-being of citizens if it does not create better livelihoods, jobs and incomes for them? The 'business case for change' must go beyond the ambition to grow the business. The business of business cannot be only business. And the 'political case for reform' must go beyond the ambition to grow the economy. Good governance must improve equity in societies.

Growth to well-being and fairness

When the meeting took place in Cleveland in 2006, there was already concern about the condition of the world. Soon after, there was a global financial crisis, triggered by an irresponsible pursuit of profits by large banks and financial corporations in the US and the UK. People wondered why hardly any of the world's best economists, who seem so confident that they have the models to explain the growth of economies and to guide policymakers, had predicted the crisis. Within the economics profession too, the dominant paradigm, of free-markets and growth first with redistribution and inclusion later, is being more strongly challenged. However, the underlying 'theory-in-use' driving the growth of corporations and economies has not changed.

According to Oxfam's and other reports, the incomes of the top 1 per cent is separated from the rest, and the wealth of the very top 0.1 per cent has drifted into outer space from the perspective of the masses below. French economist Thomas Piketty's tome on inequality, Capital in the Twenty-First Century, became a bestseller. Piketty analyses the causes for increasing income and wealth inequalities and argues that they will increase unless there is fundamental rethinking about economic policies.

After the Cleveland meeting in 2006 and the financial crisis that followed, other signs of breakdown of the global order also appeared. Refugees began flowing into Europe from Asia and Africa, driven out by political, economic and environmental collapses in their homelands. The surge of refugees has triggered the shake-up of political systems in many European countries. Liberal ideologies are under threat. The global trading system seems to be tearing apart.

There are many causes for the rise of populism, along with anti-globalization and anti-liberalization forces. The perception that the 'Establishment', of government and businesses, along with their intellectual supporters, did not care about the people below, while increasing, and celebrating, their own incomes and wealth, fuelled the opposition. 'Crony capitalism' is a phenomenon that used to be associated only with developing economies and dictatorial regimes. However, citizens in economically advanced and proudly democratic countries, like the US and the UK, are also agitated by their perceptions of collusion between governments and the rich and wealthy in their countries.

In the US, Bernie Sanders rallied a lot of support for his 'socialist' and anti-Establishment views, and Donald Trump vowed to bring back jobs to America and to drain the Washington swamp. In the UK, Brexit got support from those who felt they were being left behind while the city prospered, and the Labor Party is on an upsurge. In India, economists who had hoped Narendra Modi's government would accelerate the liberalization of the economy, which had stalled with the 'socialist' policies of its predecessor, are dismayed by the 'populist', pro-common man programmes of the government, such as the waiving of farm loans, and its reluctance to reform labour laws to make hiring and firing easier. Mr Modi has the pulse of the people, and he must have their support to win the next election.

Sales of Karl Marx's *Das Kapital* surged in the USA after the financial crisis. Mark Carney, the governor of the Bank of England (a former Goldman Sachs executive), warned that with wage stagnation and unemployment, which will increase with automation, Europe could turn to Marxism within a generation. 'You have exactly the same dynamics as existed 150 years ago—when Karl Marx was scribbling *The Communist Manifesto*,' Mr Carney noted.

However, Jeremy Corbyn and the Labor Party's ideas are more strongly influenced by another Karl, according to *The Economist*. Corbyn follows Karl Polanyi, author of *The Great Transformation*, who was part of a group loosely known as moral economists. The moral economists' critique was socialist, but in a different way to those socialists who believed that the state should play the dominant role in running the economy. They focused on something abstract and difficult to measure—the spiritual and moral decline that is said to accompany capitalism. Polanyi said liberal economists' belief that 'self-interest' is the governing principle of economies and societies was flawed. Principles of reciprocity and honour, too, have strongly shaped societies. He said that if societies focus just on market exchange and free trade, resistance (what he calls the 'counter-movement') inevitably follows.

Unlearning and relearning

Many books and articles are raising alarms about the condition of the world—the increasing inequality, the deteriorating environment, breakdowns of democratic order, geopolitical tensions, etc. These are wake-up calls, and we must pay attention to them. There are also many books that give hope, by recounting stories of change amidst the gloom, of social entrepreneurs, local community initiatives and larger movements of change. Such books and their stories are very valuable observations of both symptoms of illness and signs of change on the surface.

Then, there are other books and articles that discuss the structures beneath the surface that cause these strains to appear, such as Piketty's book. Such more 'academic' books discuss structures of economic and social policies, forms of business enterprises and the roles of technology as well as economic ideologies in reshaping these structures.

'Events', which appear on the surface, like famines, make news. However, there are also events beneath the surface, which are not as obvious. Famines can happen even if there is plentiful production of food, if the food does not reach people when they need it. The reason the food does not reach them could be that transportation facilities are inadequate or have broken down. However, people may be starving even when there is plenty of food, as well as transport, but they cannot afford to pay for it. The causes of their poverty amidst plenty could be flawed economic policies. When reports of starvation and poverty multiply and famines can no longer be seen as isolated events, and ad hoc relief measures are no longer an adequate response, there are calls for 'structural' reforms of the economy.

An image of an iceberg, with only a small portion of it visible above the waterline, illustrates a core concept of systems thinking. It is easier to see what is visible above the waterline, like the evidence of famine. Looking deeper, underwater, for its causes is harder. Yet, we must if we want to understand what below is causing the events above, as changes must be made to the structures below to reduce the frequency of events above.

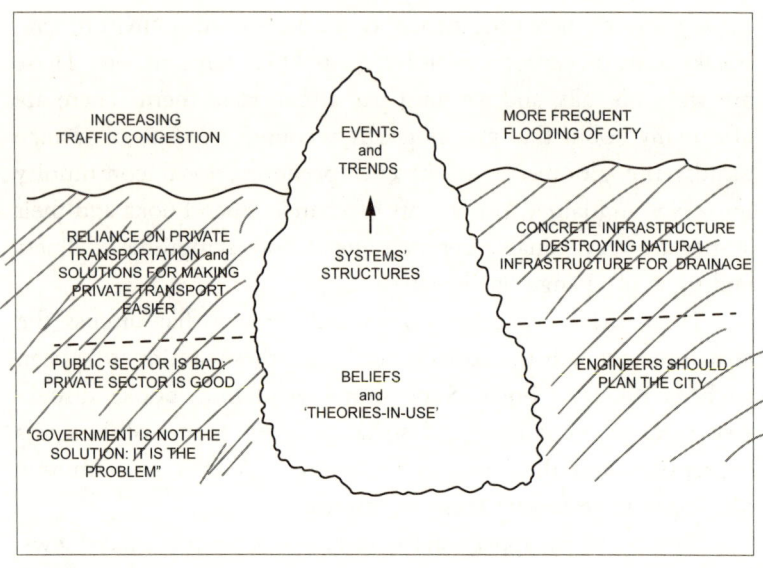

Fig 7. The Systems Iceberg

The diagram explains the concept of the iceberg used in systems thinking with two examples from city systems. Increasing traffic congestion is caused by increasing attention to the needs of private transport, which may be caused by lack of confidence in the public sector as well as by an ideology favouring the private sector. Frequent flooding in the city could be caused by blindness towards the 'infrastructure' provided by Nature and over-reliance on engineers to plan cities.

It is not possible to develop economic policies purely objectively, as some economists may like to. There are even deeper layers of the iceberg. Deep-seated beliefs and ideologies also shape our preferences for economic and social policies, not reason alone. Man-made systems, as economic policies are, can contribute to societal disharmony and environmental destruction. For example, Piketty argues that the persistent and increasing inequalities, for which he presents an impressive volume of data, are being caused by economic structures that have been pushing wealth to the top faster than it has trickled down below.

Piketty's thesis is dismissed by right-wing economists as a return to socialism, which, in their view is a bad thing. Deliberations about economic and social policies degenerate into stand-offs as soon as people label each other as socialist or capitalist, left-wing or right-wing. They must go deeper to find common ground, like the need for fairness, about which both sides may agree more easily. In short, to understand what is causing what is visible above the waterline, we must dunk our heads beneath the waterline, even though it is uncomfortable, to see the causes. We must also go deeper to try and understand the subjective ways in which we think and feel that make us prefer some solutions rather than others.

Fundamental ideas, in the backs of our heads, generally unexamined, shape our views of the world. Changing ideas at this 'paradigm' level (the expression Thomas Kuhn made famous in his *The Structure of Scientific Revolutions*) is very difficult. Kuhn explains how deep-seated beliefs, such as the story of creation and the centrality of Earth in the universe, become embedded into societies' institutions and power structures. He says that to challenge such ideas can even be life-threatening, as it was for scientists who discovered that the story of creation was a myth and that the earth went around the sun.

Yet, as Einstein said, we cannot solve problems with the same type of thinking that has created the problems. Therefore, we must consider whether there is another way of thinking about the intractable problems humanity is confronting in the twenty-first century in spite of remarkable advances of technologies—problems of persistent poverty and increasing inequality in economies, disharmony within and between nations, and the continuing degradation of our one shared planet Earth. These are the urgent matters embodied in the seventeen Sustainable Development Goals, that all nations signed up for in 2015, that humanity aspires to address.

The prevalent 'scientific' way, that has increased human abilities immensely, by developing new technologies and giving humans the ability to overpower nature, is not the best way to solve these complex systemic problems. Indeed, this way, by going too far, has unwittingly contributed to these very problems of disharmony and systems breakdown.

The scientific way grew with the European Enlightenment in the seventeenth century. A problem with the scientific way is its drive to understand the properties of individual components of a system more thoroughly in the belief that the mystery of the whole can be explained from the properties of its parts. Physicists are studying infinitesimal bits of matter hoping to understand the essence of what everything in the world is made of, and neuroscientists hope to unravel the mysteries of human thought by tracking tiny bits and bytes in the brain. Since the Enlightenment, the domains of sciences have expanded. At the same time, sciences have been breaking down into narrower specializations, each knowing more and more about less and less. Now the parts must be put together to know the whole. The disciplines must talk to each other to understand the whole. But this is not easy. The disciplines have their own perspectives and their own jargons. They cannot understand each other.

A new Enlightenment founded on 'systems thinking' is required to understand complexity—not by breaking complexity into simpler components, but by understanding patterns and relationships amongst the components of complex systems. Children are taught to think of the world in compartmentalized subjects. When they go into 'higher' education, they must focus on ever narrower subjects. When they go to work in organizations, they are fitted into narrow, functional silos. And thus, knowledge of systems as a whole is falling apart. The discipline of systems thinking has become essential to put knowledge together again, to help create more social harmony and environmental sustainability.

- Every system is designed perfectly to produce the results it is currently producing.
- Structures of systems, often invisible, cause visible events to happen. To understand trends of visible events, we must look beneath the waterline to understand the underlying structures within systems that cause these trends.
- Human beliefs influence the construction of structures and institutions within systems. Transformational change begins with examination of deeply-rooted beliefs.
- Institutions within a system are interlocked with each other.
- Institutions within a system cannot go too far in transforming themselves if they cannot bring other institutions to change along with them.
- Visionary leaders are required, who will take the first steps and bring others along.

PART C
Reorienting Our Minds

15

Taking Charge of Our Own Stories

Something had stirred deep inside Sumit after his meeting with Priya and his three college friends a year ago. Priya seemed to be following another drumbeat in her life. She seemed very happy even though she was earning much less than her college mates. She had ranked higher than them at the institute, other than Sumit perhaps, and could have gotten any of the best jobs on offer in the placement season. But she had chosen not to go down the well-beaten path.

Sumit had begun to wonder what he cared about most deeply in life. What was the purpose of what he was doing in life? He was devoting almost all his waking hours (and often sleeping very little) to produce something. But what was it? And who was all his work ultimately benefiting?

Sumit's father was a senior executive with the Tata Steel Company in Jamshedpur. Sumit's mother, a graduate from one of the country's best women's colleges, had lived in Jamshedpur ever since she had gotten married soon after graduating. There was no professional work she could do in the town. She spent her time doing social work in the poor communities around the town. Sumit's father was a very successful professional, often invited to speak at business conferences abroad. What gave his father greatest satisfaction, Sumit sensed, was the deeper purpose of the enterprise he served. It served the nation and it served the people.

The international consulting company Sumit worked with was greatly admired for its professional services. But Sumit had begun to wonder for whose good it worked for ultimately. Its clients were large companies, many of them multinationals. These large companies could afford to pay the millions of dollars of fees consulting companies like his charged for the professional services provided.

A theory driving economic growth since the 1980s was that a business' principal role in society was to increase shareholder value, and that the purpose of a business must be only business. Therefore, the success of a business, the success of its managers and the contributions of its consultants should all be measured by the amount of wealth created for shareholders. Recently, increasing inequalities of wealth within societies had begun to attract a lot of attention in the media. While consulting companies were not indicted for it, a principal cause of the increasing inequalities, it was noted, was the increase in wealth of investors and owners of companies while workers were being left behind. The French economist Thomas Piketty's book, *Capital in the 21st Century*, had received a lot of public attention. Piketty analysed the increasing distances between the wealth of the top 0.1 per cent and the wealth of the rest in countries around the world. Many reports were published about wealth and income inequality in India. The gap in India was higher than the gap in almost all other countries, and it was increasing. According to the numbers presented in these reports, Sumit was already amongst the 0.1 per cent of the wealthiest persons in India, though he was only five years out of college! Some of the partners in his firm, he reckoned, would be amongst the 0.01 per cent wealthiest people.

While Piketty's book was about society at large, an article in *The New York Times*[10] caused a flutter in the consulting industry. It was an expose of the culture and business practices of the iconic

---

[10] 'As McKinsey Sells Advice, Its Hedge Fund May Have a Stake in the Outcome', *NYT*, 19 February 2019.

McKinsey & Co. It said that partners of the firm had lost their ethical moorings in their pursuit of wealth. They had strayed from their mission of being trusted advisors of their clients towards inventing new ways of making more money for themselves. McKinsey & Co. denied the allegations. But its image was tarnished. And with it, the cultures and values of the consulting industry in general began to be questioned.

Sumit had suggested to Priya the day after the dinner that he would like to meet her again. He wondered what she cared about so much to have given up the opportunity to be as financially successful as he was. Sumit, Priya and their three friends had formed a WhatsApp group after their dinner reunion. They exchanged news nuggets and occasionally posted photos—surface-level communication only. He wanted to have a deeper conversation with Priya. He sent her a message that he was planning to come to Pune for the weekend and hoped she would be free to have dinner with him. Priya said she would be delighted.

Priya offered to introduce him to one of the local cafes, habited by young people, which she patronized, so that he could get the feel of her city. However, he urged her to join him in the restaurant of his five-star hotel where they could have a quiet chat. She was intrigued. She welcomed the opportunity to have an expensive meal she could otherwise not afford.

After they had settled down at their table, Sumit asked Priya about her work and what she had been doing since they had met a year ago. She said the highlight was the workshop she had attended at the Sabarmati Ashram. There, she had been introduced to the need for more systems thinking and more listening to make the world better. While Priya was animatedly narrating what she had learned, Sumit became very pensive. Priya was observing him. She was improving her ability to listen deeply. She had learned to listen even when she was speaking. She paused. Sumit remained silent.

Priya prompted him. 'What is on your mind, Sumit?'

Sumit began to share his misgivings about the worthiness of his work compared to Priya's. She did not try to console him. She just looked at him gently, and asked him two questions when he paused. 'What do you really care about, Sumit, if it is not your success at work? And who do you care about most of all?'

Sumit took a while to gather his thoughts. Then, he conveyed to her that he was not sure anymore. He had convinced himself that what he cared about was the success of his clients, and the success of his projects. He also enjoyed the material comforts he could afford. The problem in his mind was that while there did not seem to be anything wrong in wanting success and material comfort, and he had enough of both, there was something unsatisfying about his life. He did not have the kind of joy in his work that he sensed Priya had. He felt she was committed to a cause beyond her own success, and even beyond the success of the organization she served. Was that why she was happier than he was?

Priya nudged him a little. 'You do care for the success of your organization's clients, Sumit, just as I care for the success of my organizations' clients in the community.'

'That is true,' Sumit said. 'But the difference lies between our clients. Mine are wealthy corporations who want to make even more money. Yours are poor people who want to get a fair share in life, to be able to earn more to support their families. There is a big difference in who is benefitting from your and my good work.'

Sumit paused. There was a moment's silence. Priya did not speak. She waited for Sumit to continue.

He added, 'I have been going along with the self-justificatory economic theory, that if the rich get richer, they will invest more in the economy to make the economy better for everyone. Therefore, the rich should not be taxed much. In fact, large corporations should be given incentives to invest more, by tax breaks and with subsidies. I have helped our clients make their cases to governments for more benefits. However, after they make their investments, they are never asked how their investments helped the society that forewent its own revenues (in lower taxes and higher subsidies). The companies never ask themselves this question. Consultants are asked to make intricate calculations, with discounted cash flows, to prove how shareholder value will improve under different conditions. We are never asked to apply the same skills to calculate what value is created for society.'

Priya was hearing a deeply reflective side of Sumit she had not heard before. To support him, she said that she too was concerned about the same thing—the design of the economic system, in which poverty was not being reduced fast enough and in which inequalities were growing, with the thesis that unless the size of the pie was increased first, there would not be enough to go around. Therefore, GDP had to be increased first. India must and will become a $10 trillion economy, the prime minister says. And then everyone will be happy somehow.

Priya said that she was learning a new paradigm of good management that would improve the world for everyone, whereas the shareholder value maximization paradigm they had been taught at their institute improved the world for investors. She said that Prof. Amartya Sen, whose works she had read carefully, and Muhammad Yunus, whom she had heard at the Sabarmati Ashram, had another view of how the economy would become healthier. They said that an economy was healthier when growth was bottom-up rather than top-down. Indeed, this was Mahatma Gandhi's philosophy too. Gandhiji and Prof. Yunus had advocated models of enterprises owned by the people on the ground who do the work, rather than owned by remote financial investors in the enterprises.

She asked Sumit if he was familiar with the concept of a circular economy. He said he was. It was a way of mapping and managing all material resources through their life cycle, so that nothing was wasted.

'Right,' she said. 'That is the popular conception of the circular economy. It is about the flow of materials and energy through the economy. I want to show you my view of a circular economy. It shows how wealth is generated and flows through the economy.' She pulled out a piece of paper from her bag and made a sketch on it.

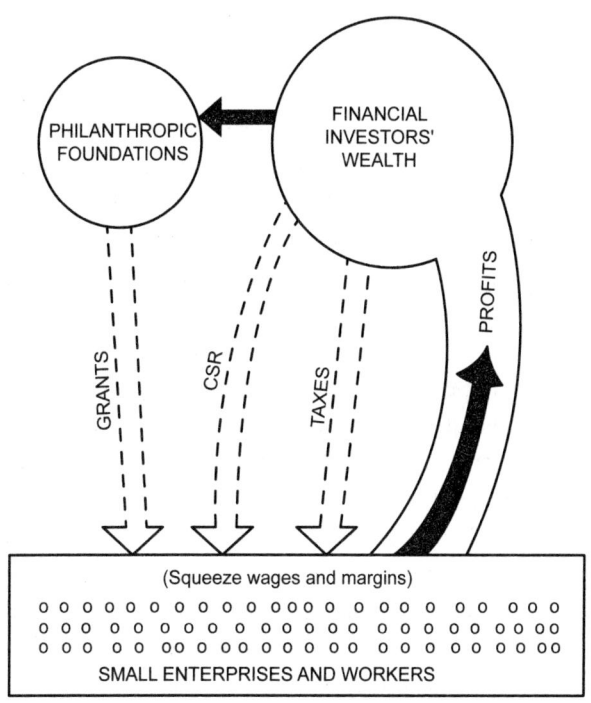

Fig 8. *The Circular Economy*

She continued, 'You remember Prof. C.K. Prahalad's concept of "the fortune at the bottom of the pyramid" we were taught at the institute. I will use the example of the shampoo sachet often used to explain his concept. Hindustan Unilever is able to sell its products to poor people by repackaging its shampoo in very small sachets, that can be purchased with very little money. Thereby, poor people get the benefit of a good product for hair hygiene, which they could not afford earlier. However, the profit from the expansion of shampoo sales is made by the investors in Hindustan Unilever, wherever they are in the world. They make the profits, not the people; their wealth is increased further.

'The issue is regarding who *owns* the enterprise? The people at the bottom, or people at the top of the economy? Unless people become the owners of their own enterprises, they will not be making any profits from the enterprises. They will not earn wealth. Those who have wealth will make more wealth by investing their wealth in enterprises to make profits. Those who have little wealth or none at all will be left further behind. Therefore, we need enterprises owned by the people and run by the people if we want to reduce income and wealth disparities. This is precisely what Gandhiji advocated and what Prof. Yunus is advocating too.'

Sumit was impressed with Priya's explanation. He said, 'I can see how the purpose of the enterprise will drive its managers' behaviour. If the purpose is to produce more profits for financial investors, then value will be extracted from others to increase the profits. In fact, this will be considered good management of the enterprise. I can see from your view of the circular economy how methods of good management that we learned at the institute, and which we are honing further in consulting companies for our clients, are deepening inequalities instead of reducing them. The pace of sucking up of wealth by wealthy investors, who can afford to pay our fees, is exceeding the pace of the trickle down.

'I see a similarity in the structures of the system of the material circular economy and the economic circular economy. In the material economy, solid waste is generated from the production system and it begins to accumulate somewhere, choking up rivers and oceans. In the circular economy, financial capital is generated out of the production system, and it has begun to accumulate in the financial sector. The size of the financial sector in economies has grown greatly in the past thirty years. Financial resources from banking are being invested in financial funds—in hedge funds, derivatives, etc. There, they create more financial wealth for investors. They do not go back into the production sector. Thus, the economic system is getting choked up by the accumulation of a virtual resource, i.e. money, just as the environmental system is getting choked by solid waste.'

'Very clever, Sumit!' Priya said. 'What do you think could be a way to de-clog the economic system?'

'My consulting company has started a new consulting practice to advise philanthropic foundations on how to produce more impact with their grants,' Sumit said. 'I have been talking to some of the consultants in this area. What is the role of philanthropy and impact investing in your view of the circular economy, Priya?

'Philanthropy and corporate social responsibility (another channel for rich corporations to "give back" to society) are good,' Priya answered. 'In fact, I rely on these channels for the small amounts of funds we need for our work since we have no capital of our own. Philanthropy and CSR are channels for "trickle down" in the economy from the big sumps of wealth that accumulate above when profits and wealth are "pulled up" from the bottom in the present economic system. These channels can only give back to the bottom some, but not much of the total wealth in the economy that accumulates above. For example, the Indian CSR law requires corporations to invest 2 per cent of their profits on CSR. The question is, how were all the profits—the 100 per cent—made.

'Taxation of the incomes of the wealthy, inheritance taxes and corporate taxes are also ways to circulate wealth back to the bottom. You have pointed out, Sumit, how well corporations argue for lower tax rates to induce them to invest in a country. The rich lobby for lower tax rates for themselves. So, the downward flow pipe is crimped. But the flow up is increased by suppressing wages and resistance to the formation of unions who could take up the causes of workers. The plumbing of the circular economy needs to be fixed for more inclusive economic growth. The solution to reduce inequalities is to increase the accumulation of wealth at the bottom, in enterprises owned and run by the people who provide their work and their knowledge to create value.'

'Wow!' Sumit interjected. 'It sounds like our consulting company. It is a partnership of the people who work in it. They make the profits and share the profits. Maybe we should teach people at the bottom how to form effective partnerships, rather than teach our corporate clients how to make more money for financial investors. The problem for us is that the people at the bottom will not be able to pay as much for our services as large corporations can. Therefore, to make more money for ourselves, we chose to serve the large corporations, not the people. Indeed, this is the problem our firm is facing while setting up the social sector practice. Not-for-profit organizations in the social sector, even the large international organizations we are focused on, cannot afford to pay as much as our corporate clients do. Therefore, the consultants and partners who work in these practices are paid less than those who work on commercial client work. Some consultants accept the reduction of pay because they care for the cause they serve. However, even they are paid very well compared to you, Priya. I admire your commitment.'

Priya deflected the praise and made an observation about the ethics they were taught at the institute. 'We were never taught to question the ultimate purpose of the enterprise we would serve,' she said. 'So long as it was a legal enterprise operating within the law, and it would pay us well, it was alright to take the job. Our job was to help this enterprise do whatever it had chosen to do more efficiently. Like professional soldiers, we must do or die, not question why.'

Sumit agreed with Priya. 'Even when we were introduced to the concept of CSR (corporate social responsibility), we were taught that CSR was good for a corporation because, in the long run, it was good for the corporation's shareholders. In other words, if responsibility for the environment and for the condition of society is not good for the shareholders then you must not do it. It is also so selfish in the end, isn't it? Unless it is good for me, I will not do it. I think the flaw is in the premise that economists have founded many of their models of economies on, that all human beings are rational and self-interested only. They do not seem to have place for people like you, Priya, and the many people you say you work with. People with emotions, and people who seem to care more for others than themselves.'

Priya laughed and said, 'Let me tell you a story I heard at

Sabarmati Ashram about Gandhiji. Some Western reporter said to him, "Gandhiji, you are the most unselfish person I have ever interviewed." Gandhiji immediately retorted, "Unselfish! Me? I am a very selfish person. I want to feel good about myself. That is why I do what I do."'

'Thank you, Priya,' Sumit said. 'That is what I am struggling with. I want to feel like I am a good person, not just a successful one by others' standards. I am a character in a story being written by others. I would like to write my own story. I must reflect on the purpose of my life.'

- Ask yourself: What do you care about most deeply?
- Ask yourself: What is the purpose of your life?

16

Two Paradigms for Managing Change

After making millions of dollars in the US and returning to India, Nishant had become deeply engaged with the cause he cared about most—finding effective ways to reduce poverty in India much faster. Poverty reduction could not be the responsibility of the government alone. Wealthy people like himself, to whom the country had given so much, must give back too. He had been educated in an IIT and an IIM. These were publicly funded, world-class institutions. The cost of his education had been very small. He had no student loans to pay off. His education had provided him the opportunity to work in the US and make a lot of money.

There were many other Indians like him, who had been to IITs and IIMs in India and had done very well for themselves in the US. Some of them felt, like him, that their money would provide greater advantage in poverty reduction, if they could support the education of a large number of professionals for the development sector. The Aspire Foundation was one of his initiatives. Another initiative, close to his heart, was a school for professional management of social development.

Management of change in the social sector was the domain of civil society organizations (CSOs). Indian CSOs were led by very devoted people. According to Nishant, their efforts were not producing outcomes on scale because their organizations did not have professional managers to manage their operations, finance and marketing functions. Four years ago, at a seminar in Mumbai, he had met a professor in development economics, Dr Sunita Deshpande. The seminar was on the subject of 'social enterprises', an emerging concept. Social enterprises apply business methods to increase incomes at the bottom of the economic pyramid, reduce poverty, and improve access to healthcare, education, clean energy, and water and sanitation. Social enterprises are expected to make up for deficiencies in the state's capabilities to provide these services to its citizens.

Sunita had been teaching Development Economics in the Pune University for many years. The Indian economy was growing fast. India was celebrated by businessmen and economists in the World Economic Forum at Davos as the 'fastest growing free market democracy in the world'. Far from the mountaintop resorts where the global rich and powerful were celebrating the growth of economies, billions of people in the world were struggling to make ends meet. Hundreds of millions of these persons were in India. What was lacking in these successful people's ideas of good economics and good business, she wondered, that disabled them from making a difference in the lives of people on the ground?

Sunita had become dissatisfied with the abstract ideas she was teaching. She wanted to get closer to reality. She got a break when an Indian philanthropist set up a billion-dollar trust and she was invited to work in a development NGO he also created. She was a member of a very small team of entrepreneurs in the social sector, charged by the philanthropist to create an organization that could produce impact on scale, applying the best ideas from the business world. They had to make sensible connections between the ideas of business and the ideas of societal development, which were not always compatible. They also had to grow their own team, to have larger impact, and find people with the right orientations to work with them. This was not easy. Young MBAs from the business world understood concepts of efficiency and good management, whereas those trained in social development did not consider those ideas as important as concepts of equity and empowerment of people.

Both sets of ideas were required and had to be combined. But how, when they seemed to come from different worlds and when their proponents spoke in different jargon. Moreover, the better 'educated' the both sides were through formal schooling, the further away they seemed to be from ground realities.

Sunita felt an urge to create a school of development management, like schools of business management, the students of which would go into the field to make a difference, just as students of management schools joined business firms and helped them improve their results. She wondered what the curriculum of this school would be—perhaps some mixture of subjects taught in business management and social development schools. She also wondered what the pedagogy would be to make the students connect with ground realities while learning academic ideas.

When Nishant and she met in the seminar, they realized they had the same vision—of developing a school of professional development management. They were coming at it from two different ends—one from concepts of business management and the other from concepts of social development. Like Nishant, Sunita was also curious about the concept of social enterprises that would apply professional management skills to improve the world for people at the bottom of the economic pyramid. Perhaps they could bring concepts of good business management and development management together.

Nishant's friends agreed to invest in the idea with him. Sunita and he began to make plans for the school. They would start small, maybe with a class of fifty at most. Finding rented premises for the school near Delhi would not be a problem. The permanent faculty would be very few, perhaps Sunita with one or two more like-minded academicians. They would supplement their teaching resources with visiting faculty—business people, consultants and social workers, with a penchant for teaching, who shared their vision of a school for development management with a difference. However, the critical issue was what should be the design of the curriculum?

Designing the curriculum

Nishant was quite taken up with the idea of 'design thinking', which was becoming very popular in business and management circles. Design thinking was permeating into policymaking as well. What attracted him about design thinking was it's out-of-the-box approach to creating new products and spaces. In the first step, a designer is required to set aside his notions of what would be good for customers. He must immerse himself amongst potential users of a product or service, to observe them and listen to them. He must open his mind and 'sense' their unmet needs. In the second step, the designer should conceive creative, out-of-the-box designs of a product or service that would meet their needs. Various techniques were provided for thinking out of the box by the many competing consultancies that were springing up to provide design-thinking services.

Nishant thought the Aspire Forum would be an ideal place to engage with potential customers of the development management school that Sunita and he were planning. The Forum's participants wanted to learn better ways to have a greater impact in development. They were a mix of people already trained in business management or in the social sciences. They were looking for something more and something different to make a greater impact. Sunita had become an active participant in the Forum's meetings. A design-thinking consultant had conducted a very stimulating workshop in design thinking for the participants. Nishant and she had agreed that design thinking would be included in the development school's curriculum.

Sunita had been reading about systems thinking. Design thinking and systems thinking seemed to have obvious similarities. However, there seemed to be something essentially different between 'design thinking', as it was being represented and applied in business circles, and concepts of systems thinking that she was being attracted to. She could not put her finger on it exactly. It seemed as if design thinking, though it required out-of-the box approaches, was embedded within the box of a conceptual theory of change. And it seemed to her that it was this theory of change that the mind must be broken out of to produce results in the development sector.

Different paradigms

Nishant and Sunita had planned an interactive session with the Forum's participants to get some inputs for the school's curriculum. The systems thinking lesson on the first day had provided a wonderful opportunity to contrast the paradigm of systems thinking with the paradigm of business management.

The thirty participants were broken into smaller groups of participants, in each of which participants with greater corporate/investment experience were mixed with others with deeper NGO/social work experience. All groups were asked to brainstorm and distil the differences between Paradigm A and Paradigm B. Paradigm A was the conventional theory of change followed in business and government, which was adopted by large NGOs too. Paradigm B was a 'systems' approach to change.

Priya, the youngest member of the Forum, was asked to distil a list of differences from the groups' reports and to present it on the third morning. This is the list Priya presented to the group.

Paradigm A: Conventional Approach	Paradigm B: Systems Approach
Group A: How to see things	
1A. Reductionist view	1B. Connective view
2A. Components	2B. Relationships
3A. Breaking apart	3B. Putting together
4A. Specialists	4B. Generalists
5A. The trees	5B. The woods
6A. One into many	6B. One from many

Group B: How to 'know'

7A. Only 'the facts'	7B. Also, the opinions
8A. Quantities	8B. Also, qualities
9A. Sizes/Scale	9B. Shapes/Scope
10A. Calculating	10B. Sensing

Group B: How to work on things

11A. Engineering	11B. Gardening
12A. Constructing	12B. Generating
13A. Controlling	13B. Catalyzing

Group C: The relationship between the change-maker and what has changed

14A. Working 'on' the system	14B. Working 'within' the system
15A. Providing a 'product' to the system	15B. Helping the system to change itself
16A. Designing a solution for the system	16B. Being a part of the solution
17A. Being 'apart from' the system	17B. Being 'a part of' the system
18A. 'Design' thinking	18B. 'Systems' thinking

Group D: Economies and Societies

19A. Markets	19B. Communities
20A. Transactions	20B. Relationships
21A. Efficiency	21B. Equity
22A. Income is a fact	22B. Fairness is a feeling
23A. Scale of the enterprise	23B. Quality of the outcome
24A. Competitive markets—if everyone looks after themselves, world will be OK	24B. Good societies—when people look after each other, world will be a better place
25A. Competitive Enterprises	25B. Cooperative Enterprises

26A. Nature is a resource for the economy	26B. Nature sustains us
27A. Consumers	27B. Citizens
Group E. Personal Orientations	
28A. Having more	28B. Being happy
29A. 'I'	29B. 'We'
30A. Competing	30B. Supporting
31A. Arrogance	31B. Humility
32A. Being noticed	32B. Noticing
33A. Speaking	33B. Listening

Fig 9. Different Paradigms

The participants were struck with the internal consistencies amongst the components of each paradigm—the lenses through which the world is observed, the relationship between the designer and the system, the structures of economies and societies, and personal orientations. This is an inherent nature of 'systems'—their diverse, constituent parts always cohere.

Together, the components create a powerful paradigm of thought and action. Thoughts guide the designs of institutions. The institutions provide channels and incentives to reinforce the thoughts. Institutions also set constraints and penalties for straying outside the boundaries of thought. Thus, paradigms of thoughts and actions become 'locked in place', and difficult to change.

Implications for the design of a curriculum of learning

Nishant and Sunitha took advantage of the deep insights the participants had collectively produced to further distil with them what must be the essence of an education to improve the world. A change in the paradigm was necessary.

They distilled three essentials to change the paradigm:

1. Systems thinking
2. Ethics of citizenship
3. Deep listening

Three changes in mind-sets to produce change in the paradigm:
- Systems thinking
- Ethics of citizenship
- Deep listening

17

Systems Thinking

An analysis of orientations essential in those who want to make the world better for everyone has revealed three orientations—systems thinking, ethics of citizenship and deep listening. A fourth orientation, 'learning to learn', will be introduced in a later chapter. Before that, let us learn more about the first three.

Systems Thinking

We are trained to specialize and to know more about small parts of complex systems. If an arborist (a specialist in trees), a botanist (a specialist in plants), an ornithologist (a specialist in birds) and an anthropologist were to go together to a forest, they would all have a fulfilling day. The arborist would note dozens of varieties of trees and estimate their ages. The botanist would collect dozens of specimens of wild flowers. The ornithologist would observe many species of birds that the others may not see. An anthropologist would inquire into the livelihoods of the tribal people foraging in the forest for products to sell. To the other three, these tribal people would appear as an interference in a beautiful natural system. Some may wish the people were not there at all, whereas to the anthropologist what may matter most of all was the condition of these people's lives, and not the condition of the forest.

Systems Thinking • 147

Like the proverbial blindmen around the elephant, many perspectives must be combined to understand a system.

Fig 10. Minds Trained to Focus on Only Parts of Complex Systems

Our minds are conditioned by years of education and practice to focus—to get to the point. If many things require our attention, we learn to attend to them, efficiently, one by one, giving each our undivided attention as far as possible.

On the other hand, systems thinking requires that many disparate things must be kept in mind at the same time while attending to any one of them. This is because what we do with one will affect the others also. Therefore, our efficient fixes of one part of a system can backfire onto another and may cause the whole system to collapse. Thus, a surgeon operating on the kidney must keep in mind that the body has other vital organs also, and that inadvertently damaging the liver, or heart, while heroically fixing the kidney, may result in a dead patient with a good kidney.

Systems thinking is the art of keeping many things in mind at the same time so that the patterns of relationships amongst them can be seen. It is the relationships amongst the parts of the system that give the system its systems' level abilities. Such systems' level abilities cannot be perceived by examining each part separately. X-rays of the toes, knees, hips, back and MRIs of the brain of Usain Bolt, the multiple gold medal-winning 100 meters' sprinter, cannot reveal why he can get his whole body across the winning line much faster than anyone else. He is an amazing sprinter because the connections between the parts of his body and the internal flows of information amongst them work very smoothly. The mind is trained to zoom in and focus on the parts, whereas systems thinking requires the mind to zoom out, to see all the parts together and to closely observe how they interact with each other.

The Club of Rome predicted, in its seminal report, *The Limits of Growth*, in 1972, that population growth as well as economic growth were putting great pressure on the Earth's ability to provide the resources required for human consumption and industrial growth. They pointed out that Earth has processes for renewing itself—for replenishing and cleaning its water sources, for circulating carbon through the ecosystem, etc. They also explained how faster economic growth was putting great pressure on the Earth and interfering with the Earth's ability to renew itself. Destruction of forests—to provide timber raw material, or to layout plantations to produce economically useful palm oil and rubber, or to clear land to build cities—reduces Earth's capacity to capture carbon through trees and so carbon builds up in the atmosphere. Tapping underground for water to feed agriculture and for human consumption damages natural aquifers that took millions of years to build.

The Club of Rome pointed out that while each of the activities was necessary for human development, the combination of all these activities was destroying Earth's ability to sustain human development. Economists, industrialists and technologists seemed to have lost sight of the fact that human activity was a part of a larger system. In economists' growth models, the natural environment was an 'externality'. In business models, Nature was only a passive resource providing commodities for industrial growth and a dumping ground for the wastes produced by industrial (and human) activity.

The Club of Rome introduced concepts of systems thinking into public discourse. However, systems thinking has remained a sideshow to the dominant, non-systemic approach of scientific progress. Now, with alarms of climate change and concerns about persistent ill health of societies (with increasing inequalities and divisiveness), the need for systems thinking and systems action has become imperative.

The systems thinker, Donella Meadows, the lead author of the Club of Rome's report, explains why systems thinking must use the language of pictures rather than the language of words. Words and sentences, she points out, 'must by necessity, come only one at a time in linear, logical order. Systems happen all at once. They are connected not just in one direction, but in many directions simultaneously. To discuss them properly, it is necessary somehow to use a language that shares some of the same properties as the phenomena under discussion. Pictures work for this language better than words, because you can see all parts of a picture at once.'[11]

Donella Meadows also pointed out that 'every system is perfectly designed to produce the outcomes it is presently producing'. The many, diverse parts that constitute the complex system are interacting in ways that are producing the outcomes it is producing. Therefore, to understand why the (undesirable or desirable) outcomes are being produced, one must understand the structure of the system as a whole. For example, stripping out politics from an economics model, because politics is too messy and unquantifiable, will result in incomplete models that cannot explain why economic policies are adopted under 'populist' or 'nationalist' pressures, even though they are irrational and stupid to an economist.

In one of the previous chapters, we have noted the need to understand 'three models' of systems, before one can help the system improve itself. The first of these is a model of the system as it actually is. Since a system is composed of many disparate sub-systems and components, all of which must be seen together to understand the structure of the system, one should begin with a picture of the system.

---

[11] *Thinking in Systems—A Primer*, Donella H. Meadows, Chelsea Green Publishing, 2008.

Getting started

Put up a big sheet of paper. On it, write everything that appears to be an important part of the system, even if one does not yet know rationally what role it plays in the system. When mapping a complex socio-economic-ecological system, it is essential to include perceptions of persons with different viewpoints—people who see the system through the lenses of different scientific disciplines, people within the system with different historical identities that give them unique cultural lenses (and blinkers), and people with different economic circumstances.

Ask each of these persons to say what they consider important. Display everything on that big piece of paper, so that everyone can see the system through others' perspectives. Let people hear why others consider whatever they have posted as an important part of the system. Then let the group step back and see the whole forest with everything that is in it, and not just the birds, the trees, the flowers, or the people eking out livelihoods. Do not limit yourself to just the economy, society or the natural environment. Let everyone see everything together. The first step of creating a picture together with other diverse people of the system as it is, is when the paradigm of systems thinking is switched on. An integrative picture is laid over the parts seen by specialists.

A picture with diverse parts scattered in it may not make any sense. It begins to make sense when the relationships between the disparate components are explored. What goes with what. What causes what. What is caused by what. Some components may seem to have an affinity with each other and can be seen as a cluster of some deeper forces. Some of these forces may seem to have obvious cause-and-effect relationships with each other. When components are clustered together and lines of interaction between the components and forces are added to the picture, a pattern emerges. The underlying structure that gives the system its 'systemic' ability can become visible.

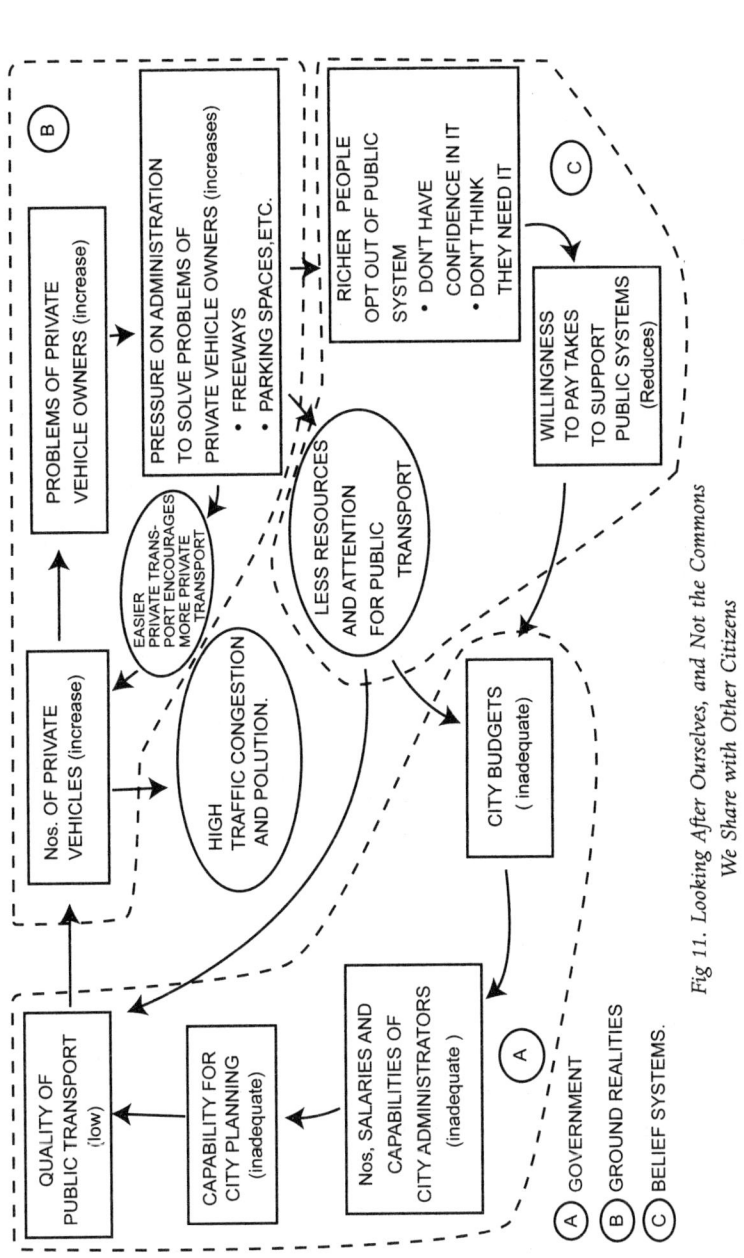

Fig 11. *Looking After Ourselves, and Not the Commons We Share with Other Citizens*

Consider this picture put together by the citizens of an Indian city. They were concerned about the increasing levels of pollution and the chaotic traffic in their city. Some believed it was a failure of the city government. Others felt the principal cause was undisciplined citizenry, while some others were convinced that the problem was incompetent city planning. When they put all their views together, they began to see the incompleteness of their understanding of what makes city systems work, and to see interconnections amongst their views.

The first step of systems thinking is to visualize complex phenomena as a system. With the preparation of a rough picture of the system with connections amongst its components, the light bulb of systems thinking has been switched on. It is not complicated. Semi-literate villagers in India have been able to make good systems' maps of their village systems, in which they have included their knowledge of how economic transactions happen and how power flows in decision-making in their communities, along with mapping of the physical and natural infrastructure of their village. Children are wonderful systems thinkers. They are curious. They see strange similarities and connections before they are taught how to separate the things they see into different categories.

The paradigm of systems thinking, as a way of seeing and understanding the world, is easily learnable—even by uneducated village people and children. It is more difficult for those who have been educated for too long to use the reductionist, 'split-it-into-specializations' and 'quantities are facts qualities are opinions', scientific approach.

When experts from many disciplines come together to try and make a shared picture of a complex system, of which they know only a small part, they should try, as a first step, to put their ideas, in simple, jargon-free words, into one big visual picture. It is remarkable what insights they can then collectively get into the structure of a complex system. I have seen the light bulbs switch on many times in experts' minds, whenever they have allowed themselves to do something as 'childish' as standing before a big whiteboard to put their thoughts as sketches in a bigger systems picture.

An example of this process, of putting diverse heads together to get a systems' view, was the examination, in 2012, of why the Indian economy was not growing faster and, more importantly, why the growth was not inclusive and so much environmental damage was being caused by Indian's rapid economic growth. The Government of India wanted to make an economic growth plan. To make a good plan for the future, it was necessary to ascertain what the present state of the system was, and what were the forces that were impelling new policies, as well as the forces resisting them.

Many diverse stakeholders' views were brought together. The principal forces operating within India and external forces affecting the country were mapped in a systems diagram. It revealed insights into changes required in the architecture of policies and institutions to rebuild trust between citizens, the government and business. The erosion of trust was disabling the capacity of the system to move in an aligned manner, and everyone, including business, was suffering from the policy confusion and paralysis. The poorest people in the country were suffering the most. Institutions of both government and business would have to reform themselves to earn the citizens' trust and ease the increasing political logjam in the governance of the country. It made visible the root cause for the declining growth rate of the economy, which lay inside the sociopolitical system, and which could not be found from looking merely at graphs of GDP, inflation and investment rates.

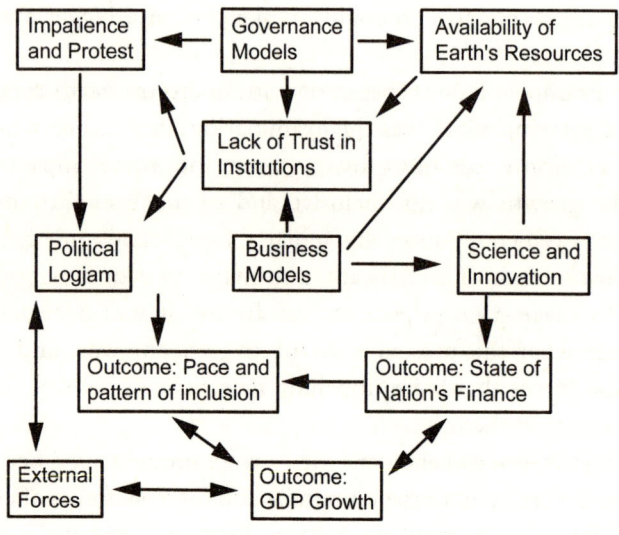

Fig 12. Leverage Points for More Inclusive Growth

Learning to think systemically is like learning to swim or ride a bicycle. Reorienting one's own instinctive behaviour to suit a new form of activity is the first step that is necessary. In swimming, one must learn to breathe differently when one is in water compared to how one would breathe outside it. In cycling, one must learn to balance one's weight in a different way compared to when one is walking. Once one is able to breathe in water, or to balance on a bike, one can do many other things to improve one's proficiency. If one is learning to swim, one can learn different strokes. If one is learning to cycle, one can learn to ride faster and to take sharp turns.

Similarly, in systems thinking, the first step is critical, of reorienting one's mind to include many diverse components together, and to focus on the relationships amongst them, by first making a rough systems picture. Thereafter, one can learn many more tools and techniques of systems thinking to improve one's proficiency.

Systems thinking is as old as the hills. It is native to people on all continents who live close to Nature. They instinctively understand that they are a small part of a large system, which nourishes them, and which, in return, they must take care of. The advent of the scientific Enlightenment in Europe in the seventeenth century enabled Man to increase his power over Nature.

The European Enlightenment enabled Western civilization to roll over traditional civilizations of the East. It gave Europeans more technological, economic and military power than others. The scientific paradigm broke systems into pieces. It harnessed the power within atoms, and the power of bits and bytes of information. Now systems thinking is required to put it all together again, to save Man from his own self-destructive power.

The ability to keep hold of the bigger picture, to collaborate across different perspectives, and to be very aware of their own place and role in the system, comes more naturally to some. Do Asians think differently than Westerners? Psychologist Richard E. Nisbett reports the conclusions of tests conducted by him and other psychologists. He explains their findings in his book *The Geography of Thought: How Asians and Westerners Think Differently and Why*. The studies indicate that to Asians the world is 'a complex place understandable in terms of the whole rather than in terms of the parts', and 'subject to more collective than personal control'. Whereas to the Westerner, the world is 'a relatively simple place, composed of discrete objects that can be understood without undue attention to context' and is 'highly subject to personal control'.

Though an Easterner myself, I have learned science and management in the ways of Westerners. I expect that readers of my book will have a similar outlook to knowledge. Therefore, it is easier for us to connect to systems thinking through the language of people like us, who think scientifically, rather than to go straight back to the wisdom of the I-Ching, Tao and the Vedas.

An elegant introduction to the methods of systems thinking, for people like us, is provided in the *Fifth Discipline Fieldbook*, edited by Peter Senge and his colleagues.[12] The *Fieldbook* says, 'At

---

[12] Currency Doubleday, 1994.

its broadest level, systems thinking encompasses a large and fairly amorphous body of methods, tools and principles. All oriented to looking at the interdependence of forces, and seeing them as part of a common process.' In the *Fieldbook*, my former colleagues in Innovation Associates, Jenny Kemeny, Michael Goodman and Rick Karash, as well as Donella Meadows, explain the tools of 'systems dynamics', one of the schools of systems thinking developed by Professor Jay Forrester and his colleagues at the Massachusetts Institute of Technology (MIT). Jenny, Michael, Rick and Peter Senge were all at MIT, and they developed simple techniques, with which people could apply the principles of systems dynamics to analyze the systems' pictures they could make by listening to many diverse views.

Readers interested to explore the deeper philosophical and scientific underpinnings of systems thinking will find *The Systems View of Life: Unifying Vision*[13] well worth their time.

When practising systems thinking:
- Include many perspectives to draw a systems picture
- Think together about what the relationships amongst the various parts could be

A summary of concepts and tools for systems thinking introduced in this book:
1. The relationships amongst the constituents of a system matter as much as the constitution of the components (Chapter 10).
2. The shape of a system matters more than its size (Chapter 10).
3. Focusing too much on the here and now, we miss the connections between systemic causes and effects that can be widely separated in space and time (Chapter 10).
4. Three types of systems: Engineered Systems, Self-adaptive Systems and Chaotic Systems (Chapter 13).
5. Prevalent 'theories-in-use' (paradigms of thought) are also forces

---

[13] Fritjof Capra and Pier Luigi Luisi, Cambridge University Press, 2014.

within the system that shape it (The Iceberg) (Chapter 14).
6. The contrast between the widespread paradigm of engineering systems from outside with the paradigm of a self-adaptive system with everyone including the designer within it (Chapter 15).
7. Along with a system's components and their relationships, the 'purpose' of the system determines its behaviour (an idea introduced in Chapter 13, which will be developed further in Chapter 17).

18

Ethics of Citizenship

An ethical orientation is necessary to distinguish between the 'smart' thing to do and the 'right' thing to do, and also, the difference between 'being good for others' and 'doing well for oneself'. An action may be technically correct, legally correct and the most effective way to produce an outcome. However, these tests are insufficient to make an action an 'ethically' correct action.

What would be tests to determine whether an action is an ethical action? This is the question that David, a successful, young computer scientist, working in an AI laboratory in San Francisco, who we met in Chapter 5, had begun to ask himself. His friend, Jenny, a researcher in cultural psychology at Berkeley, had given him an essay to read. From it, David had obtained some important insights about what ethical principles are, and how they are learned.

He had learned the distinction between ethical principles that can be discovered by reason and ethical principles that are imbibed, as faiths, by being a citizen of a community. He found the metaphor of 'the rider and the elephant' a very good one. He began to see differences between individualist moral codes and socio-centric moral codes. Individualist moral codes focus mostly on the rights of individuals. Socio-centric model codes also add on the obligations of individuals to the societies in which they live. In an individualistic moral code, causing no harm to others, and fairness towards others, are the basic principles for one's conduct in society.

In a society-centric moral code, loyalty, respect for authority and sanctity (respect for the society's traditions and taboos) are very important too, as they maintain social stability.

Haidt provides an anthropologist's view of how ethical principles evolve within communities and societies. Howard Gardner, the eminent American psychologist and professor of cognition and education at the Harvard Graduate School of Education at Harvard University, provides another view. Gardner is well known for his theory of multiple intelligences. In his book, *Truth, Beauty, and Goodness Reframed: Educating for the Virtues in the Twenty-First Century*,[14] he provides insights into how ethical principles are learned in professional institutions.

Gardner highlights the pervasive growth, in the last century, of professionally managed institutions such as modern, business organizations. With the spread of industrialization, the communities in which many people spend most of their lives and learn their values are such professionally managed organizations. People are not born into these organizations—they join them later in life. Moreover, people spend a large number of their post-adolescent, formative years in education that prepares them to do the work they will be required to in such organizations. They learn technologies and management skills to work in business corporations or to set up their own. If they are studying to become doctors, they learn the technologies of medicine and professional medical practice. Whatever their profession, they learn the technical and professional skills required to produce results efficiently. They learn what is technically correct to do, and legally acceptable too. Whether they are doing ethically correct things or the organizations they work for are doing ethically correct things are not matters they are trained to dwell much on.

David's conscience was stirred when he realized how much harm social media, which had been touted as a saviour of democracy and a promoter of social harmony, was causing

---

[14] Howard Gardner, *Truth, Beauty, and Goodness Reframed: Educating for the Virtues in the Twenty-first Century*, Basic Books, 2011.

democracy and societies. Social media and technology companies had risen to the top of stock market leagues. They were creating enormous wealth for their investors. But this did not prove that they were 'good' companies. He was beginning to wonder what distinguished a good company from a merely successful one.

The purpose of the enterprise

Donella Meadows, the systems thinker, says a system is composed of three constituents— elements, relationships and purpose. The first two constituents of a system were explained in the previous chapter. Let us now consider the third—the purpose of the system.

A large number of good, honest men can be organized in a hierarchy, with clear lines of command. They could be a large organization to provide relief to people in distress. The discipline within the organization, as well as the devotion of the men to their duties and their willingness to take great risks in their own lives to help save those of others, enables a relief-giving organization to perform very well.

An army of soldiers trained to kill their enemies is also a large, disciplined body of good, honest men, organized in a hierarchy. Soldiers, too, are devoted to their duties. They, too, are willing to give their lives to fulfil the purpose of the organization. However, the purpose of their organization is to threaten and cause harm to their enemies, not to provide them succour.

Both, relief-giving organizations and armies trained for war, have similar elements, and similar relationships. However, they have very different purposes. When confronted with life-and-death situations, soldiers in an organization for war and soldiers in an organization for relief will follow different ethical rules as the purpose of an enterprise shapes the ethics of the people in it.

Let us consider then, what is the purpose of a social media enterprise? For that matter, what is the purpose of any media enterprise, whatever technology it may use for communication— whether it is the Internet, television or print on paper?

I was a participant in an Aspen Institute seminar, in Aspen, Colorado, in July 2002, where the question of what the purpose of a business is became vivid. The seminar, on the challenges of global capitalism, was conducted by philosopher, Michael Sandel, author of *Democracy's Discontent: America in Search of a Public Philosophy* (1998) and the bestseller *What Money Can't Buy: The Moral Limits of Markets* (2012). In the seminar, Jerry Levin, CEO of Time Warner, chaired a discussion on the role of the media. Many participants expressed their anguish at the 'dumbing down' of discourse on mainstream media. Discussions on TV had deteriorated into gladiatorial contests, such as the hugely successful American show at the time, *Crossfire*. The participants asked Levin how citizens would be engaged with the deeper issues of their societies if all they saw and read in the media was designed only to entertain them? Did the media not have a responsibility as a pillar of democracy, to engage and educate citizens about relevant issues?

Levin explained why the media must focus on the demands of its readers and viewers. He said the media was a business, and a good business must give its customers what they wanted. If they wanted more entertainment, then the media must give them good entertainment.

A participant in the Aspen Seminar said that society could not allow business leaders to get away with the justification that they were giving the people what they wanted. 'Many people want hard drugs. There is a lot of money to be made by supplying hard drugs to these customers. Could a business that supplied hard drugs be defended on the principle that it was giving people what they wanted? Just as sellers of drugs are declared criminals, all business leaders must be held responsible for the bad effects of their products and services on the lives of people,' she declared.

All businesses must be held accountable for the impacts their products have on the lives of their customers and on societies. Generally, developers of products are the first to know, when they test their products in the course of development, about the potential harm their products could cause. Sadly, they often suppress this knowledge in the rush to sell their products and make profits. Tobacco companies have done it. Pharmaceutical companies have done it too. Promoters of social media companies have rushed in with new technologies and made great wealth for themselves.

Sean Parker, the founding president of Facebook, broke his silence in October last year, telling a conference in Philadelphia that he was 'something of a conscientious objector' to social media. A month later, *The Guardian* reports,[15] Parker was joined by another Facebook objector, former vice-president for user growth, Chamath Palihapitiya, who said, 'The short-term, dopamine-driven feedback loops that we have created are destroying how society works. No civil discourse, no cooperation; misinformation, mistruth. This is a global problem. It is eroding the core foundations of how people behave by and between each other. I can control my decision, which is that I do not use that shit. I can control my kids' decisions, which is that they are not allowed to use that shit.' Psychologist, Adam Alter, author of *Irresistible*, an examination of technology addiction, says, 'Many tech titans will get up on stage and say things like: "This is the greatest product of all time", but when you delve you see they don't allow their kids access to the same product.'

Trust in business leaders has been declining according to the Edelman Trust Barometer, an annual survey of citizens' level of trust in institutions and their leaders. Some leaders in the business world have realized that businesses cannot carry on the way they have, taking shelter behind the ideology that the business of business must be only business. Laurence D. Fink, founder and chief executive of the world's largest investment firm, BlackRock, has spoken up. BlackRock manages more than $6 trillion in investments. Mr Fink has written to the leaders of all the firms BlackRock is invested in, that their companies need to do more than make profits—they need to contribute to society as well if they want to receive the support of BlackRock.

---

[15]'Never get high on your supply—why social media bosses don't use social media,' *The Guardian*, 23 January 2018.

The world needs business leaders who are not merely innovators with new ideas and good builders of organizations that 'scale up' the impact of the innovations. Leaders with new ideas and abilities to execute must also have the capacity to reflect on the ethical question about the purpose of their enterprise.

Developing an ethical orientation

Business schools have so far focused mostly, if not entirely, on teaching their students better methods for managing and getting things done, with the purpose of the enterprise taken for granted as the maximization of profits. They are being pressed now to teach ethics to their students. Ethical decisions require an application of principles, which may conflict in practice. Therefore, an ability to understand the specific context in which the principles have to be applied is as necessary as the knowledge of the principles.

Ethical choices are generally very difficult. For example, there is the 'utility' question that philosophers have debated over centuries. Should the needs of a few be sacrificed to provide the maximum benefit for the maximum number of people? There is also the difficult question of the rights of individuals versus the needs of communities, which complicates policies when rights for privacy clash with needs for collective security. Ethical problems often require trade-offs between two good principles. And there are no absolute answers to difficult ethical questions.

The case study method is used in business management schools to compel students to reflect on the trade-offs that executives must make in the difficult decisions they have to take in real life while striving to grow their businesses. Too many case studies focus on the impacts of decisions on the revenues, profits and shareholder value of the company. Too few, so far, have posed the ethical dilemmas that boards and CEOs must confront if corporations are to be good citizens of societies. What if the dilemma is whether to immediately withdraw a product or service that makes most of the company's profits, when its harmful effects become known to the management and there is no alternative product to replace it? How many professors of marketing, finance or business strategy prompt their students to take the ethical decision regardless of the large impacts it will have on the business' financial health?

Corporate citizenship

Institutions are the vehicles with which humanity achieves its aspirations. The limited liability corporation is an invention of man—a device created to attract capital. The liabilities of investors are limited to encourage them to invest and take risks with their capital. The East India Company, established in 1600 AD, was one of the first 'limited liability corporations' in the world. Its owners contributed capital for the voyages of the company's ships to the East and, later, for its ventures in India. The owners shared the profits of the ventures amongst themselves.

The records of meetings of the East India Company's Board in London in the seventeenth and eighteenth centuries reveal that the directors were only concerned about calculating the profits and their distribution amongst the shareholders. They hardly seemed aware of the violence and corruption in the conduct of their employees in India. The tenet driving the conduct of the East India Company was 'the business of business must be only business'. The rest was none of their business. The resentment of India's people to the conduct of the East India Company led to the War of Independence in 1857. Combined with the reactions to the conduct of the East India Company of high-minded societal leaders in Britain, this resulted in the British Government taking over the Company's affairs in India.

However, the principle that 'the business of business must be only business' has continued to guide corporate conduct into the twentieth century, especially in the Anglo-Saxon world. It was reinforced by the philosophy of Nobel Laureate Milton Friedman and the Chicago School of Economics. The responsibility of the board of a company, according to this philosophy, is to ensure that shareholder value is increased and that disbursement of profits to the shareholders is equitable.

Ted Nace, in an excellent book, albeit with a provocative title, *Gangs of America: The Rise of Corporate Power and the Disabling of Democracy* (2003), says that Abraham Lincoln had a premonition in 1864 after the American Civil War. Lincoln wrote:

> I see in the future a crisis approaching that unnerves me and causes me to tremble for the future of my country. As a result of the war, corporations have been enthroned and an era of corruption in high places will follow, and the money power of the country will endeavor to prolong its reign by working upon the prejudices of the people until all wealth is aggregated in a few hands and the Republic is destroyed.

Over the next 150 years, through a series of legal and ideological battles in the USA, corporations acquired all the rights of citizens to protection of property and other freedoms. In addition, they obtained privileges of limited liability that human citizens do not have. Laws were made whereby corporations could privatize and internalize profits while costs of damages to communities and the environment were socialized and externalized.

Corporations, who claim constitutional rights as 'citizens'—rights to property, freedom of speech, and the right to sue—have been using their enormous financial power to protect themselves against common citizens, and even against governments elected by these citizens. Common citizens are too small, individually, to stand up for their rights against corporate power. Therefore, workers form unions and consumers form associations and sue corporations with class action suits. Corporations have successfully lobbied for US laws that have weakened the powers of unions, and that have limited the impacts of class action suits by consumers. On the international stage, large investors have lobbied for rights to sue elected governments, in courts that will stand apart from the Supreme Courts of nations, if they make laws or take other actions to protect the rights of their citizens, which may harm the rights of investors who are not even citizens of those countries.

'All citizens are equal,' George Orwell wrote cynically in his prescient book *1984*. 'But some citizens are more equal than others.' Clearly, business corporations have become more equal than human citizens in democracies.

New forms of ethical business enterprises

The most profound ethical questions that all spiritual traditions in the East and the West ask every person to find answers to are:

- What is the purpose of my life?
- What is my role in the larger system of which I am a part?

These are the questions that troubled Arjuna on the eve of the battle at Kurukshetra in the great Indian epic, the *Mahabharata*. The Bhagvada Gita—'the song spiritual'—is Lord Krishna's guidance to Arjuna.

The Golden Rule in every religious tradition is: 'Do unto others as you would have done unto yourself.' It enjoins each person to consider the interests of others before taking any action. What the wisdom of the ages, around the world, says to us is that selfishness must not be the driving principle for guiding one's conduct. Actions driven by self-interest alone are unethical.

Business corporations are institutions designed to fulfil a purpose. If the business of a business enterprise is defined, self-referentially, as only business itself, the enterprise must serve only its own interests. Such selfishness in a human being would be considered immoral and unethical in all religious and spiritual traditions. However, within an economics' view of the world, in which every human being is presumed to be only a self-interested person, an institution whose purpose is to pursue only its own interests, is acceptable. Indeed, it is admired for how effectively it can fulfil its self-interests, increase its own profits and increase the wealth of its own shareholders.

The context in which corporations must now operate is

changing. An increasing awareness of fundamental human rights, as well as realization that economic activity is damaging the environment too much, has begun to put moral pressure on corporations to change their ways. Society has begun to demand a new code of business responsibility in return for granting corporations their licences to operate. The business of business can no longer be just business. A new, more ethical form of business corporation must evolve, responding to the need for better corporate citizenship,

A simple definition of a social enterprise is an enterprise that produces environmentally friendly products or socially useful services such as affordable education and healthcare. There are profits to be made at the bottom of the pyramid by providing these services. The question is, who makes the profits—the investors, or the people who buy the products and services? When the conventional business model is applied to the production of socially desirable products, the people pay and the profits flow up to investors, whose wealth increases. This does not help poor citizens to increase their wealth or build their own capabilities. When the performance of managers of such business enterprises, merely cloaked as 'social enterprises', is evaluated within the conventional business paradigm, their managers deserve handsome compensation.

Impact investing has become a fashionable way for wealthy people to 'give back'. However, the principal purpose of many is not to 'give back'—they are broadening their investment portfolios to get more returns for themselves. It comes back to what is the purpose of the enterprise and what is the purpose of making the investment. If the purpose is indeed to make the world better, then the principal measure of the performance of a social enterprise must be the benefits it provides others, especially those least well off in the world. It cannot be the size of the organization and its budgets or the profits it makes.

An argument against using impact as the principal measure of performance is that impact is difficult to measure. Many of the desired outcomes of societal development programmes, such as improvement of equity in society, are hard to quantify. Moreover, since many factors contribute to such systemic conditions, it is not possible to attribute improvement in them to any one intervention. Therefore, it is recommended that more easily measurable and preferably quantifiable indicators should be used. Amongst these, the amount of financial resources deployed and the numbers of persons formally engaged with the work are easiest to quantify, and these measures of inputs become surrogates for the enterprises' impact. However, when inputs become confused with outcomes, the enterprise can lose sight of its purpose.

Objectivity and insight must not be confused with data analytics. As was explained in the earlier discussion of systems, nothing should be left out of an assessment merely because it cannot be quantified. Systems thinking can help to map the multiple causes and effects within a system. It can provide insights into what can be done to improve outcomes, and what must be observed to assess how the system is functioning, even if it cannot be quantified.

The Noble Eightfold Path is one of the principal teachings of Buddhism. The path begins with practices of right mindfulness, right view and right intention. The other five practices are right concentration, right speech, right action, right effort and right livelihood. The Eightfold Path provides the right ethical orientation for individuals and business corporations too.

Right Mindfulness: Always be mindful that you are a small part of a larger system that nurtures you. And, be mindful that you are not the engineer of this system and cannot be:

Right View: A systems view.

Right Intention: To nurture and support the system of which you are a part; not to extract more for yourself at the cost of the system.

- Systems are composed of elements, relationships and a purpose.
- Any organization (or individual) whose purpose is only to serve itself cannot be an ethical citizen of society.

19

Deep Listening

His Holiness the Dalai Lama says, 'Listening is the first of the three wisdom tools in Buddhist tradition, the other two being contemplating and meditating; it is the gateway to improving oneself, both mentally and physically. Listening without preconceived notion and with respect and full attention, is the way to understand each other. This is the way to communicate on issues without distortion.'

Listening is the discipline necessary for achieving right mindfulness and right view, the first two of the eight pathways in the Noble Eightfold Path of Buddhism. Our personal histories provide us with lenses through which we see the world and with which we evaluate others. The members of the Aspire Forum in the master class on systems thinking had realized that listening to other viewpoints is necessary to understand systems fully.

For example, an economist and a sociologist surveying a bazaar will notice different things. The economist will note the buzz of transactions and circulation of money, and the haggling over prices. The sociologist may pay more attention to differences between what men and women do in the market and also the ways in which owners of shops and their employees relate to each other. The economist and the sociologist may be of the same race, the same religion and the same age too. However, their different academic disciplines provide them with different lenses to see reality.

Listening deeply to another is necessary to understand others' viewpoints and their ethical principles, as David realized when he was with his parents at Thanksgiving. It is not easy though. 'Preconceived notions', as the Dalai Lama points out, come in the way. To listen deeply to another person, we must go behind the hard veneer of stereotypes, which we paint over them, preventing us from seeing the real persons behind our mental stereotypes.

Why is listening difficult? There are four reasons:

- We confuse 'listening' with 'hearing'.
- We are taught in schools and colleges to excel in speaking rather than listening.
- Our minds have coping mechanisms to manage an excess of information beyond what our minds can process at one time.
- The ubiquity of information with which we are being bombarded with the Internet and social media is making it much harder to listen deeply.

When a teacher demands that students pay attention and repeat what she just said, she is making them hear her. Teaching, according to a joke at the MIT campus in the 1990s, is the process by which information goes from the notes of the lecturer to the notes of the student, without going through the minds of either. Students are hearing a lot. But are they listening to the patterns beneath the information they are receiving? Are they noting the questions arising in their minds? If a teacher were to ask her students after giving them some new information, what they thought about it, rather than repeating it, she would understand what is going on in their minds and encourage the students to listen to their own minds.

Students are taught to speak and write clearly. They are hardly ever taught the art of listening. Leaders in organizations are taught the skills of public speaking—of getting their points across to people effectively. TED talks are very effective one-way expositions—however, there is no interaction with the audience, no listening to each other. On social media, we must learn to make sharp, attention-receiving statements in 140 characters. It is always about how to speak effectively to be heard, not about how to listen to others.

Nobel Laureate poet Rabindranath Tagore makes a prayer, in his poem *Gitanjali*, for a world of freedom in which, 'The clear stream of reason has not lost its way in the dreary desert sand of dead habits'.

Just as an AI programme develops algorithms to improve its efficiency in processing information, our minds develop mental habits, i.e. mental algorithms, to process information very fast. Our minds need this capacity so that they can take quick decisions when they must. For example, should one 'fight or flee' when faced with an unfamiliar situation. The minds of all animals, including human beings, have this capability. What enables the mind to think fast is its store of stereotypes and categories. When it sees something new, it quickly compares what it sees with the stereotypes in its mental store and judges into what category it falls. Is this a dangerous animal or a harmless one? The judgement must be made quickly—to fight or to flee—because it could be a matter of life or death.

In addition to the capacity to 'think fast', human minds also have a capacity, greater than other animals, to 'think slow', in the words of Daniel Kahneman, who was awarded the Nobel Prize for his work on the psychology of judgement and decision-making. It is the capacity to think slowly and to reflect that enables human minds to develop a deeper understanding of the world.

If some muscles in the body are used more often, they become stronger, and others, which are lesser used, remain weaker. A rower has very strong arms and shoulders, whereas a cyclist has very strong legs. Similarly, If the parts of the brain that are used for thinking fast are used much more, they become much stronger, while the reflective parts of the brain are neglected and weaken. This is the pernicious effect on the human mind of the ubiquity of information provided by the Internet and social media.

The Internet, social media and mobile phones bombard us with millions of bits of information, messages and tweets. It is difficult for anyone to keep in touch with everyone and everything. If we are connected, we suffer from an 'attention deficit disorder'. The resulting coping strategies are to remain online all the time, pay shallow attention to many things and choose the many we wish to follow from the millions we can. All these strategies make a deeper understanding of others impossible.

Being online all the time with shallow attention reduces the depth at which we are with others. When people meet to have coffee together, everyone is looking at their smartphones, and not at each other. People at a business meeting keep one eye on their smartphone or iPad on the table, and the other to dip in and out of what is happening in the room. The Internet and social media provide vast 'reach' to people everywhere. However, staying connected all the time, so that we do not miss out on chatting with people, reduces the 'richness' of the conversations among people. Platforms on the Internet have made information abundantly available and for free. It has become an ocean of 'water, water everywhere, but not enough good water to drink'. A lot of chatter, but what is the insight? A lot of noise, but what is the signal?

To cope with the floods of information, we choose websites, tweeters and Facebook friends, which makes us stay in touch with people we like because they are like us. We easily understand what they say. We are locked within our own 'conceptually gated communities'. Thus, the 'world is broken up into fragments by narrow domestic walls'—another line in Tagore's *Gitanjali*.

Listening deeply

David, the AI scientist, realized that he was not listening to his father. He had come to the conclusion in his mind, albeit with some evidence, that his father did not have the same views about politics as he had. Therefore, in the very divisive political atmosphere in the US, David had placed his father permanently on 'the other side'.

When he had, for once, inspired by the essay Jenny had given him, removed the screen between the 'thinking fast' and deep listening parts of his mind, he had learned something new. He had learned something about the structures of US institutions that he had never thought about. He had also learned to respect his father more.

David noted that there are three levels of depth in listening. Shallow listening is only hearing *what* is being said. It receives the data that the speaker is providing. For the next deeper level of listening, the listener turns on his reflective mind. He wonders *why* the speaker is saying what he is saying. What are the reasons in the speaker's mind? Great listeners have even deeper curiosity. They wonder how the speaker has developed his beliefs. What is the speaker's history? Deep listeners are really curious about *who* the other person is.

Discussions, debates, deliberations and dialogue

Discussions amongst people can be conducted in many different formats. There are debates, deliberations and dialogues, and there are cacophonies. A cacophony is the default format into which discussions will descend unless they are structured and managed in one of the other formats. The free-for-all melees on Indian TV shows, in which everyone is yelling and no one is listening, are cacophonies, though their organizers describe them as 'debates'. We use the terms, debates, deliberations and dialogues very loosely. However, each of these forms of discussion has a purpose and rules for its conduct to enable it to fulfill its purpose.

A cacophony on a TV show, in which there is only speaking and no listening, is designed for entertainment. Viewers like to see people pummeling and insulting each other, and so the TRPs of such shows are high.

A 'debate' is described by Webster's dictionary as 'a contest in which the affirmative and negative sides of a proposition are advocated by opposing speakers'. The purpose of a debate is to determine who is right and who is wrong. In debates, the opponents listen to each other's arguments carefully with a view to trip each other. Debaters do not debate with the intention to learn something new and to change their own views. They debate to win.

Deliberation is a process which brings together various opinions. It promotes the use of critical thinking to weigh the pros and cons of different options. The purpose of a deliberation is to gather all the facts and opinions, and to enable people to see the larger picture. Deliberations demand that people listen more deeply, to understand others' points of view, and to enquire into why they think the way they do, rather than to immediately find what is wrong in their view. Deliberations are required for participants to see the whole picture of a system.

Dialogues go deeper than deliberations do. Dialogues require that people listen even more deeply, to understand 'who' the other person really is behind the stereotypes in our minds about them. Dialogue amongst people who believe they are not like each other is required to create more harmony in a world being 'broken up into fragments by narrow domestic walls'.

Reorienting our minds

Tagore prays for 'a heaven of freedom in which the mind is without fear and the head is held high', in which, 'tireless striving stretches its arms towards perfection'. To progress towards this heaven of freedom, we must develop new orientations of systems thinking, ethical being and deep listening. Orientations cannot be taught with lectures. They are internal disciplines developed with practice. They are learned, not taught. The challenge faced by deans of business schools and schools of development management (such as Nishant and Sunita) is how to design their schools' curriculums and pedagogy to enable students to develop these orientations.

Howard Gardner, the eminent professor of cognition and education at Harvard University, discusses this in his book, *Truth, Beauty, and Goodness Reframed: Educating for the Virtues in the Twenty-First Century*. He recommends that students should keep journals with their reflections and their questions, and note their intentions and plans to learn. With their personal journals to assist them, they can listen to themselves, and learn to learn.

> 1. There are three levels of listening: to the *what*, the *why*, and the *who*. Purposes and formats for discussions include:
>   - Cacophony for entertainment
>   - Debates to determine who is right and who is wrong—who is the winner.
>   - Deliberations to gather and understand different perspectives
>   - Dialogues to promote an understanding of each other amongst people who may not appear to be like each other
> 2. Mental habits cannot be changed by lectures; the mind needs to retrain itself to acquire a new orientation.
> 3. Personal journals can be a useful tool for people to observe the patterns of their own thoughts, and thus, listen to their own minds.

20

Networked Organizations

The SDGs are inspiring many people around the world. Problems such as persistent poverty and inequality, poor health and environmental degradation that the SDGs aim to solve are systemic issues. Systemic problems have multiple interacting causes. They are not amenable to 'silver bullet', technology or policy solutions. They cannot be resolved by any one actor.

Philanthropists, with wealth accumulated from corporate investments, are 'giving back' to society in programmes aligned with the SDGs, and so are business corporations through their CSR (corporate social responsibility) programmes. When corporations get to the ground, they realize the need for partnerships with NGOs who have local knowledge. Large, international NGOs, working on any issue around the world—such as the care of children, the concerns of the elderly, or the protection of the environment—also know that they must work in partnership with local communities.

All stakeholders recognize the need for effective partnerships. However, disagreements amongst stakeholders, as well as amongst diverse experts with divergent perspectives, who must come together to address complex issues, make progress difficult. The default theory of effective management—of command-and-control—becomes very tempting to apply. Governments construct centralized top-down programmes. Corporate CSR, as well as international NGO programmes, are managed centrally to achieve scale and improve efficiency by deploying best practices.

There are three problems with this approach. The first is 'one-size does not fit all'. The second is that the many different capabilities that must be brought together to address systemic issues are unable to collaborate with each other easily on the ground when all of them, whether in government, an international NGO, or a global philanthropy, are 'reporting up' to their respective bosses at their centres. The third problem is that the people who must be the ultimate beneficiaries of the solutions and who can contribute significantly to their design and implementation, have inadequate voice in the design and management of expert-driven, top-down programmes.

The Club of Rome warned in 1972 that humanity would face a 'Tragedy of the Commons' if it persisted with its paradigm of economic growth. Its warnings were largely ignored. Since then, more reforms within the prevalent paradigm enabled long periods of economic growth around the world. Meanwhile, systemic problems of environmental degradation, climate change and economic inequities got worse. The SDGs are a realization that humanity cannot postpone much longer the development of new strategies for the management of the commons.

The history of humanity's progress is a history of evolution of institutions that have enabled societies to achieve what they want. New forms of institutions of business, such as the limited liability company invented in the seventeenth century, enabled capital to be accumulated more efficiently to grow economies. Innovations of elected parliaments of the people enabled the implementation of ideas of democracy that societies began to aspire for since the sixteenth century, first in small pockets in Europe and North America, and then in a flood by the twentieth century.

The Tragedy of the Commons is caused by the clash of two sets of rights, along with two fundamental principles of good governance. The fundamental principle driving democracy is human rights. Every individual, rich or poor, has a right to fundamental human needs such as health and education, and to equal political rights in the governance of their societies. The fundamental principle driving the growth of capitalist economies is the right to private property, which is consonant with a concept in economics that human beings are self-interested agents who take care of only what they own. These two principles lead to very different principles for the governance of enterprises. In democratic governance, every human being, even if she/he owns nothing, must have equal voice. In capitalist enterprises, those who own more (e.g., shares of a company) must have proportionally more weight in governance.

A new Strategy for the Commons is required to stop the unfolding Tragedy of the Commons. Faster progress towards the SDGs will require new models of enterprises, in which many agencies must collaborate, and in which the people have a much greater say in governance.

Ravi, the CEO of the large, successful company we met in Chapter 2, was facing a dilemma. His heart told him that the measures by which business analysts were gauging his company's performance were too narrowly focused on the financial returns that investors wanted. The analysts seemed unconcerned about the impacts the company's products may have on the health of people, or the impacts the company's production and distribution processes may be having on the environment, or the impacts the company's business processes may be having on the governance of society.

With the increasing demands from citizens to hold corporations accountable, some analysts have become concerned about corporate managers' capabilities to manage risks. However, the risks analysts are concerned about are the risks to the company's own profit streams, not the risks to the health of people and societies.

While Ravi cared deeply about the condition of the people, he felt trapped within a large system of institutions in which the parts were interlocked. He could not change his own part, even if he wanted to. Other parts would have to change too. The deans of business management schools in the Cleveland conference (mentioned in Chapter 15) felt they too were in a bind. They felt they could not change what they were teaching their students unless the customers of the business schools—business corporations and consultancies—changed what they were paying for. If corporations and consultancies wanted to recruit students who knew how to increase a company's revenues, profits and shareholder value, business schools would continue to produce them.

The board of the organization for the elderly, with which Henry and Nancy worked, was looking for a new form of organization to bring together diverse partners in their quest for a better world for the elderly. The question they had was, what organizational form should the new collaborative arrangement adopt to fulfil its shared aspirations and to achieve outcomes on scale?

An imperative to 'scale up' has become widespread in development circles. There are many successful stories of transformational change. However, each of them is very small in comparison with the magnitude of changes required to meet the SDGs. Therefore, there is a demand for 'scaling up'. But there is confusion between scaling up 'outcomes' and scaling up 'organizations' to achieve the outcomes.

Henry's board of trustees was exploring the differences between three forms of organization:

- The conventional organizational form with central control which is adopted by business corporations, governments, and also by large civil society organizations.
- A 'network' of organizations.
- A 'movement' for change.

A good engineer or a good manager must choose the right instrument for the job to be done. Organizational forms are instruments. Different purposes require different forms of organizations.

Economies of scale; economies of scope

A large, unitary organization can produce economies of scale. Costs are reduced when the same product or service is produced on a large scale. Economies of scale are obtained by standardizing products and production methods. 'You can have a car of any colour car you want, so long as it is black,' Henry Ford said. By ruthless standardization and by production on a large scale, he reduced the cost of automobiles to make them affordable to his factory workers and other persons who could not have bought a car otherwise.

However, there are many products and services that perforce require many diverse components to be brought together in varied combinations to produce the outcomes desired. Most of the SDG challenges are complex issues that require customized, local solutions, as was explained in the previous chapters. Complex development challenges require many capabilities to be brought together in different combinations to fit into different contexts. They require a form of organization that produces 'effectiveness through scope', not 'economies with scale'.

When they were sitting by the pool in Hanoi, Henry had explained to Nancy the difference between organizations that coordinate their parts and people through organizational structures and systems that force compliance, and organizations in which people coordinate with each other because they are committed to achieving the same goal.

Movements

Movements are examples of people moving together, creating energy on a large scale, to overcome conservative forces resisting change. The Indian Freedom Movement, the Civil Rights Movement in the US, the Arab Spring uprising in Egypt and the MeToo movement are all examples of movements for change. People are not formally recruited into these movements. They do not have any job descriptions. Nor are there any formal performance reviews and financial incentives. Yet people are willing to give a lot—even their lives sometimes—to help achieve the goals of the movements. They are like a tide of water, composed of billions of water particles, which by moving together in the same direction, can break down walls. Movements dissipate when the goal is achieved. When the tide breaks the wall, it breaks up too, and loses its energy. The movement has served its purpose.

What must be done next, and what form of organization is required for the next task to be done? This was the question that Mahatma Gandhi had proposed for the leaders of the Congress Party, who had led India's freedom movement, to reflect on in early 1948, soon after India had obtained its independence from a century of British rule on 15 August 1947. The record of the discussions in this meeting, which was held in March 1948 in Sevagram, after the Mahatma's death, has been published in 2007 in a book, *Gandhi is Gone. Who Will Guide Us Now?* edited by his grandson, Gopal Krishan Gandhi and Rupert Snell.

The 50 participants in this meeting included Jawaharlal Nehru, Rajendra Prasad, Maulana Azad, Jayaprakash Narayan, Acharya Kripalani, Sucheta Kripalani, Zakir Hussein, Rajkumari Amrit Kaur, Vinobha Bhave and Kamalnayan Bajaj. The need of the hour in March 1948 was for a strong government. The British had hastily divided the country and departed. With their exit, the edifice of government and even the vaunted army in India that they had commanded, had to be divided into two. And all this on the agenda was amidst the holocaust of the Great Partition. Therefore, the creation of strong organizations to govern the country and assure security was uppermost in the minds of Nehru and many others. Other urgent problems, of having enough food to feed millions, and enough jobs to provide them incomes, also festered in the minds of the participants.

The question Gandhi had raised, about the role the Congress party would play in India's future, was also discussed. Should it be a political party only? Or should it be an organization for social work—a gigantic NGO, as it were? Should it have two wings—one for its political work and the other for its social work, and what would be the relationship between the two?

Networks

Vinobha Bhave made a case for a new form of organization unlike the hierarchical organizations necessary for government, political parties and large businesses. It would be a network of volunteers (and voluntary organizations). He explained that only such an organization could preserve the spirit of service to others, whereas hierarchical organizations would dissipate energies in internal matters and power politics. Acharya Kripalani supported Vinobha's argument. Others in the meeting, while recognizing the need for a non-hierarchical form of organization, wondered how activities organized in the loose manner Vinobha Bhave proposed could ever be 'scaled up' to have a large effect. They discussed several ideas but could not find a satisfactory solution.

The challenge of finding ways to coordinate thousands, perhaps millions, of individual initiatives without an excessive centralization that would kill their voluntary spirit, confronts all business, government and political organizations when they expand. They centralize to coordinate expanding activities. But in the process, they invariably smother the yearning in people for freedom to do their own thing, and to stand up for their own cause rather than do what they are told to do. Therefore, there is a desire for other forms of organization in which people can coordinate with other like-minded collaborators without any bosses to make them work together, and in which they serve because they care for the cause rather than the financial compensation and hierarchical authority that conventional organizations offer as rewards for good work.

Henry had described to Nancy the pernicious effects on the cultures of NGOs when they scale up, with the mistaken belief that it would be necessary for them to become larger to achieve outcomes on a larger scale. What is required to achieve large scale outcomes, without having to scale up the organization itself, is an organization form in between, on one hand, the conventional, Weberian form of organization, which is the default mode adopted by business, government and civil society organizations when they scale up, and, on the other hand, the very loose form of a movement. What is required is a form of organization with more structure than a movement, but less rigidity than conventional organizations. What is required is an organization form that does not lose the power of commitment to an aspirational cause while obtaining sufficient efficiency through compliance with a minimum set of rules that all its members will adhere to.

Before we examine what the nature of these connections are, we should clarify the difference between a 'platform' and a 'networked organization':

Platforms

A platform enables multiple parties to transact with each other efficiently. Visa provided a platform for merchants, customers and banks to make money transactions with each. By reducing transaction costs and easing transactions amongst them, it provided benefits to all of them. The Internet has provided a platform on a much larger scale to carry out a large variety of digitizable transactions amongst people and organizations. On the back of the Internet, Amazon has created a platform with enormous reach for commercial transactions. Social media platforms, also on the back of the Internet, enable exchanges of information amongst people in many forms—words, pictures, videos and sound. However, the platform itself is neutral to what its users intend to do with it. It does not care if a collection of people uses it to run a business in pornography, or a terrorist network, or a movement to save the planet. Indeed, this is the ethical problem that owners and managers of social media platforms are now being accused of neglecting.

In a networked organization, as we will define it, its participants have a collective purpose to come together. Members of a networked organization are in the same network if they subscribe to its purpose. What binds them is their collective purpose, whether an evil one or a charitable one. Even though a platform can enable transactions of information and money amongst them to be conducted more efficiently, what bonds members of networked organizations are shared goals and values.

Networked organizations need structures to combine the efforts of their members. These structures should not be as rigid as those in conventional organizations. Yet, they must enable the collection of many to become one to advance towards their goal, whether it be the alleviation of poverty in a poor district in India, or the care of the elderly everywhere in the world. A networked organization of members who come together voluntarily and are driven by their commitment to a common cause, must not be, and cannot be controlled from outside itself. It must set its own rules. It has to govern itself. It must be a 'self-adaptive' organization.

The model of a complex self-adaptive system described in Chapter 13 provides a framework for the structures of a networked organization driven by a purpose. They are:

- Aligned aspiration to set the direction.
- Permeable boundaries within the system, and with the wider system too, to enable cooperation.
- A minimal set of critical rules for equitable and efficient transactions amongst members.
- A flexible resource pool with requisite variety and sufficient redundancy.

Governance of the network to maintain these structures would require processes for:

1. Affirmation of the shared, aspirational goals of the members.
2. Periodical inquiries by the members of (a) the condition of the boundaries between them: are they adequately permeable; (b) the efficacy of their internal rules—which ones should be dropped and what new rules should be added, and (c) the composition of the network's internal resources: should other members be enrolled to provide the scope of capabilities the network needs.

3. An articulation, following these inquiries, of the practices that will be adopted, and the behaviours that will be discouraged to improve the effectiveness of the network to meet its goal

Questions that invariably arise as networks evolve are: who are the 'members' of the network? Who selects them? How will they know they are members? These questions seem very important from the conventional view of an organization, whereas, in the concept of a network that Dee Hock had successfully implemented in Visa, it was, 'a network of free agents, none of whom understand the whole of the network nor do they need to, but each of whom knows the ground rules for participating.'

---

1. Large, conventionally structured organizations provide 'economies of scale', whereas complex, systemic challenges require organizational forms that produce 'effectiveness through scope'.
2. Conventional organizations coordinate through compliance; whereas movements and networks coordinate through commitment.
3. Networked organizations are less rigid than conventional organizations, and have more structure than movements.
4. A networked organization is united by its purpose.
5. Platforms can provide a facility for members of a networked organization to conduct their interactions.
6. Self-governed networks can convert systems thinking into systems action.

21

Learning to Learn

One is reminded frequently that 'The only constant is change'. What has changed though is the pace and pattern of change—it is more dynamic, faster and less predictable. VUCA has become a trendy managerial acronym. It is short for volatility, uncertainty, complexity and ambiguity.

Another trendy word in business and policy circles is 'innovation'. Like salt that must be added to most dishes, it seems that innovation must be mentioned in all management presentations. VUCA and innovation go hand-in-hand. The more the world changes, the greater the need for innovation. And, the greater the number of innovations, the more the world changes!

Introducing another acronym, one may say that predictions cannot be made in an IVI (Innovation- VUCA-Innovation) world. Since managers are expected to get things done efficiently and to meet targets predictably, the IVI world presents fundamental challenges to the very concept of 'managing'.

There is an urgent need to rethink the curriculum of education institutions. An increasing lack of trust in business institutions, the demand for more accountability for environmental and societal sustainability, and the rapid changes in technologies, shapes of industries and the content of work, are compelling schools of business management and development studies to go back to the drawing board. It has become a huge challenge for business management schools everywhere. This was also the challenge before Nishant and Sunita who were designing the curriculum for their new school of development management.

Teachers of management and managers of management schools have an existential challenge. Unlike general educational institutions whose purpose may be to prepare young people to be good citizens, business schools are expected to equip people to create wealth and earn money. They are judged by how much wealth their students create and how much they earn. Therefore, they must predict what the shapes of industries and jobs will be in the future and equip their students accordingly.

They are caught in a double bind in an unpredictable IVI world. Their students cannot know what skills and knowledge they will need in the future, and management schools cannot know precisely what to teach them that will remain useful.

In an IVI world, life's course cannot be sharply separated between a short period of intense education followed by the rest of one's life in which the benefits of the education are reaped. In an IVI world, the only useful knowledge without a short shelf life will be the ability to be a good learner throughout one's life. Therefore, all educational institutions must develop their students to become better learners. Students must learn to learn, and teachers must go back to school to learn to learn too!

Educational institutions are not the only institutions that must learn to learn within a dynamically changing environment. Business organizations must learn faster than their competitors in a dynamically changing world. The process of economic development is a process of countries developing competencies so that they do not have to govern themselves more effectively. They must learn to do what they could not do before. The process of evolution in Nature is a process of species learning and acquiring new competencies within a very complex evolving system.

Indeed, the only sustainable competitive advantage a business enterprise or a country may have in an IVI world is the competence to learn and change faster than any potential competitor.

How do complex systems learn to learn?

Learning to learn in the business world

Useful insights on how business organizations learn to learn faster than their better endowed competitors can be obtained from the history of Japan.

The Japanese economy was shattered during World War II. Japan's cities and factories were bombed to smithereens. When the war ended, with the formal surrender by Japan in September 1945, the victorious Americans dismantled Japan's industrial conglomerates. Nevertheless, within twenty-five years, Japan's economy rose, like a phoenix from the ashes. And by the 1980s, Japanese companies in many industries—steel, chemicals, automobiles, home appliances and music systems—had become world-competition beaters and had expanded their businesses around the world. From being producers of cheap, low quality products, Japanese companies and their products had become the hallmarks of quality.

People from around the world came to Japan to learn what had caused the Japanese industrial miracle. Japanese industrial organizations and people in them had learned to do what they had not been able to do before, and they had learned to do it better than organizations and people in other industrially advanced countries. During those years, companies in Western countries had not been resting on their laurels. Spurred by competition amongst themselves, they, too, had been developing new products and had been improving their production and marketing processes. However, the Japanese, coming from behind, had overtaken them. The Japanese had proven that they were better and faster learners.

The searchers for the secret ingredient in Japan's success found something quite simple. It was the relentless focus within Japanese organizations on the process of learning. Embedded inside the Total Quality Movement, which had transformed Japanese industries, was the concept of the Learning Cycle. The four-step framework of the Learning Cycle was applied by teams of workers on the shop floor to eliminate waste and improve reliability of their own work processes. The framework was also applied by managers to guide the development of new products and new markets.

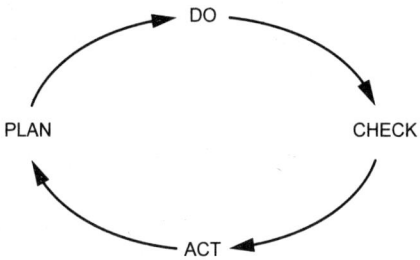

Fig 13. The PDCA Learning Cycle

The Learning Cycle has four steps. In the first step—Plan—a plan is made to achieve the intent the workers or managers have in mind. In the second step—Do—the plan is implemented. There is nothing unusual so far. Planning and doing is what all managers are expected to do. The third step in the Learning Cycle is Check. This is when learning begins to be explicitly inserted into the cycle. The doers are required to pause periodically and to reflect together on what they have accomplished so far. They must ask themselves, honestly, whether they have achieved what they had intended to. And if not, why not? Was the flaw in the plan they had made, i.e. what they had chosen to do? Or had they misinterpreted what was happening in the world around them, and had the world changed in ways they had not anticipated when they made the plan.

From these reflections arise new insights into what is happening around them, as well as insights into their own behaviours. These insights must then be applied in the fourth step of the PDCA Learning Cycle—Adjust. The team must note its new insights about the world around it, adjust its plan and improve its actions. Thus, the team must go iteratively through the Learning Cycle, repeatedly, in a process of continuous learning and continuous improvement.

Learning to learn in the development world

Three professors from the John F. Kennedy School of Government at Harvard University (all of whom have also worked in the World Bank) have combined their insights into what is required to scale up development outcomes and improve public services in countries that have longer ways to go to achieve the SDGs. Matt Andrews is a professor in government (public financial management and budget reform); Lance Pritchett is an economist; and Michael Woodcock is a sociologist. They bring an inter-disciplinary perspective to issues of development.

In their book, *Building State Capability: Evidence, Analysis, Action*,[16] they recommend a process of problem-driven iterative action (PDIA) for speeding up production of outcomes on the ground, simultaneously with the building up of capabilities of the state along with other actors, to produce these outcomes. They say that doing and learning-to-do cannot be separated. The construct of the PDIA process they recommend is very similar to the PDCA Learning Cycle explained before.

Learning to learn in Nature

Nature is an enormous, complex, 'self-adaptive' system. It is a system with many sub-systems and species in it, all of which also are self-adaptive systems. They 'self-adapt' and evolve the capabilities they need to survive when the environment around them changes.

'Sense and respond' may be the most basic way to describe the process of action learning of insects, animals, and even chemical substances. They sense something in the environment and respond to it. It is also an elementary description of the process of learning.

Children are natural learners. A child learns about the world by poking at things and observing their reactions. However, a child's mind begins to go further. She wonders why the object reacted

---

[16] Oxford University Press, 2017.

the way it did. She may try to open up the object. Or she will experiment by changing the way she pokes the object to see what then happens. Thus, a very basic representation of a learning cycle consists of four steps—sense, respond, observe and then adjust the response (SROA)—repeated iteratively. It is similar to the plan-do-check-act (PDCA) learning cycle. With each cycle, knowledge is improved and the action is sharpened too.

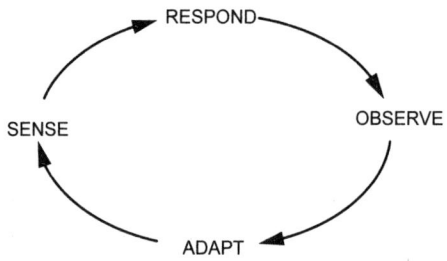

Fig 14. The SROA Learning Cycle

Though seemingly similar, there are two significant differences between SROA and PDCA. PDCA does not seem to give a prominent place to 'sensing' before planning. The other difference is in the splitting of the response step in SROA into two steps in PDCA—Plan and then Do, whereas, in natural systems, responding seems to flow instinctually from sensing.

Design thinking

The emerging discipline of design thinking is often described as a three-step process of insighting, creating and prototyping. The first step, corresponding with sensing in SROA, requires a designer to immerse herself, with an open mind, in the real world of potential customers. From this open-minded exploration fresh insights may emerge. Then, in the next step, creative responses may be conceived to these insights. After this, physical prototypes must be produced to make the ideas tangible and testable. Prototyping and testing in design correspond to the Check step in the PDCA cycle.

I will now describe a comprehensive learning to learn cycle by combining the essentials from the four learning frameworks—PDCA, PDIA, SROA and design thinking. It cycles through four steps.

1. Sensing/insighting
2. Creating/visioning
3. Prototyping/experimenting
4. Reviewing/adjusting

The fourth step feeds back into the first step to complete the iterative learning cycle.

When the participants in the Aspire Forum (in Chapter 15) had compared the conventional paradigm of management with a systems approach, they felt that design thinking as was being taught and practised in the world of business was different to systems thinking which was necessary for achieving the SDGs.

I will now place the three learning disciplines discussed earlier in the book—systems thinking, an ethical orientation and deep listening, into this four-step framework of learning to learn, and we will also compare design thinking and systems thinking tools for each step.

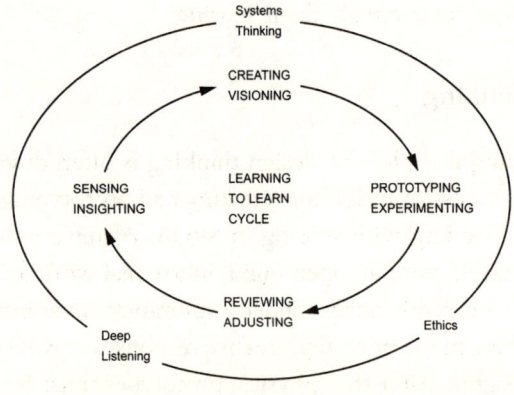

Fig 15. *The Learning To Learn Cycle*

1. Sensing/Insighting

Both design thinking and systems thinking give great importance to the first step. Design thinkers are urged to immerse themselves in the real world of potential customers, without preconceived notions, to sense unmet needs. Systems thinkers are also urged to see the world through many diverse perspectives and only then to put together a view of the system.

Both design thinking and systems thinking require deep 'listening' without prejudice in the first stage. The difference at the sensing stage between the two may be in the scope of the system being explored, and therefore, the diversity of the people to be listened to. The recent surge of interest in design thinking has arisen from the business sector, where there is interest in developing new products and services for customers. Therefore, design thinkers' explorations may be focused on a smaller set of potential customers and stakeholders, whereas development systems thinkers must explore broader societal systems.

The more significant difference is the application of systems mapping tools in systems thinking. The toolkit of systems thinking has tools to analyse and to visually present the connections between diverse forces in the system. Application of systems thinking tools in design thinking will improve the quality of design thinkers' insights.

Systems thinkers use the image of an iceberg, most of whose mass is below the waterline, to explain the power of systems thinking. They say that conventional approaches to data gathering collect information about what is visible above the waterline, whereas, deeper forces of emotions, prejudices and biases, that make people do what they do and think what they think, are not visible. They can be explored only by going beneath the waterline into others' perspectives, which requires deep listening.

Deep listening is the essence of a dialogue as explained before (Chapter 18). It enables people to understand the viewpoints of people who are 'not like us' and we do not agree with. Dialogic processes enable very deep insights into the forces causing conflicts in societies. They can enable people to understand their own biases and observe the mental filters they unconsciously apply which limit their understanding of others. Dialogic processes are tools for very deep learning about the world. They can provide insights also into who 'I' am.

2. Creating/Visioning

The next stage of designing is to produce an innovative idea to meet the unmet needs sensed in the first step.

Robert M. Pirsig poses a fundamental question in *Zen and the Art of Motorcycle Maintenance*.[17] Writers are taught rules of good writing. But he says that it is not sufficient to produce a great essay or book. The beauty of a great essay lies not only in the quality of the writing, but also in the idea the writer is expressing. But where does the idea spring from, Pirsig asks. Creative (or innovative) ideas seem to arise magically in creative flashes. Once the idea is there, it can be given a good shape—with the skills of good writing if it is a book, or the skills of the mechanic if it is a machine.

Creative ideas are more likely to emerge when the analytic left brain is stilled. 'Sleep over it', is good advice when the mind is struggling with a complicated problem for which a solution is not clear. Many techniques have been developed to suspend left-brain thinking temporarily, marketed by creativity labs and consultants in design thinking. Such techniques make the mind temporarily 'unlearn' by shaking it out of its habits, and they clear mental space for fresh ideas.

In product design processes, the new idea may be visualized in the mind of an individual designer, whereas in the processes of social change, where diverse actors have to shape the future together, the new idea must be a shared vision. Therefore, visioning must be a collaborative process when designing social change with new institutional arrangements.

Stakeholders must listen to what other stakeholders care about

---

[17] 40th Anniversary edition, Vintage, 2004.

to create a shared, aspirational vision to guide the next steps to take together to bring about the desired change. The process of listening is necessary in this step in institutional design processes also.

3. Prototyping/experimenting

'Out of little acorns, big oaks grow.'

A new idea when it forms may seem attractive in the mind. However, it is fuzzy and needs to be fleshed out so that it can be seen better. When it can be seen more completely and concretely, one can also test it and evaluate how it might work in the real world. The building of prototypes and experimenting with them is an essential part of processes of design and innovation. If the idea is the seed, the sapling that grows out of it is the prototype. One can now visualize a tree.

'Give the sapling a chance to build its strength before you start pulling at it to see how strong it is', is a rule recommended to designers and innovators. One can imagine many reasons why a new idea will fail. There is an anxiety to check too soon if it will work and if it is worthy of being invested in further. When the idea begins to take shape (the sapling appears), it behoves the entire team to concentrate on how to make it work rather than evaluate why it will not work. In other words, strengthen the idea before you put it to test.

Product and service ideas can be prototyped to test more easily than can ideas for institutional changes. Nevertheless, prototyping is essential in processes of societal innovations also before they are rolled out on a larger scale. Major improvements have been made to processes of designing complex physical products such as automobiles and airplanes with application of computer-aided design and testing. The need for physical prototypes is greatly reduced. The prototype can be visualized on a computer screen and it can be manipulated and subjected to digital tests. The design can be altered and significantly improved before a physical product is final, and ready to be put to use.

Scenarios

The equivalent in the social world of prototypes in the physical world are 'scenarios'. Scenarios are descriptions of what shape the system can take if certain forces in it prevail. They are sketches of what the world could become, not predictions of the future. Scenario thinking (which is an outcome of systems thinking) works with shape scenarios, rather than range scenarios that economic and business forecasters use. Range scenarios describe the consequences of different levels of a critical variable—such as oil prices or GDP growth, whereas shape scenarios describe alternative shapes the system can take with combinations of various forces. Range scenarios presume that the structure of the system will remain basically unchanged, whereas shape scenarios, which are formed from an analysis of the structure of the system, can project fundamentally altered conditions of the system.

Scenarios formed from systems thinking provide 'wind-tunnels' through which 'what-if' ideas about particular forces can be mentally tested. Thus, scenarios derived from systems thinking are a powerful tool for prototyping and experimenting when designing social and institutional change.

4. Reviewing/adjusting

The fourth and last step in the learning cycle feeds back to the first step. It is a very critical step, and a very difficult one too. At this stage, the strength or weaknesses of an idea is revealed, and its success and failure can be judged. However, not only is the idea judged, people who promote the idea feel judged too.

The US Army instituted the practice of 'After Action Reviews' in the 1990s as part of its programme to become a faster and better 'learning organization'. After any significant military action, the leader and the participants were required to sit down and reflect about what they could learn. Some suggested questions were:

- What had we set out to accomplish?
- What have we actually achieved?

- What did we think we knew about the environment when we made our plan?
- What do we know about the environment now?
- What has contributed to the gap (if any) between what we set out to do and what has been achieved?

The purpose of these broad questions was to stimulate a blame-free introspection about why the variation came about, and not who was to blame for it.

In the second chapter of the Bhagavad Gita, Sri Krishna advises Arjuna: 'You only have a right to the work, and not to the fruit thereof.' In other words, success or failure of a project should not trouble the doers. In practice, it is very hard to avoid feeling blamed for failure even if no blame is ascribed, or to avoid wanting appreciation for success. Participants find it hard to avoid insinuating blame or avoid crediting individuals for the success. Emotions are always present. Rules for conducting good dialogues can help to manage these undercurrents and improve the effectiveness of after-action reviews.

Going deeper and broader

While journeying through the steps in the learning cycle, the disciplines of systems thinking and deep listening and dialogue enable travel at deeper levels.

Systems thinking

Systems thinking and deep listening (and dialogue) are essential for change in social systems and environmental systems, and for changing embedded institutional arrangements. Whereas industrial design systems work in the realms of customers and products and services, social and environmental systems operate in the realms of citizens and institutional arrangements.

Both, product (and service) systems, and societal and

environmental systems, operate in a 'market' of exchanges—of give-and-take. Markets for products and services, in the customer-and-business realm, operate in realms of things that money can buy. Citizen-and-society systems must operate in markets for needs that money cannot buy, where fairness and equity, and justice and dignity, are values whose increase is the outcome desired, not only monetarily measurable values of financial profit, shareholder wealth and GDP of nations.

Intangible values such as dignity, justice and harmony are not easy to quantify—and perhaps lose their essence when dried into quantities. Yet, they must be included in an analysis of the forces that shape the world. Improvement of the quality of these values must be a principal objective of design of social systems and institutions. Systems thinking and 'shape' scenarios enable the inclusion of such unquantifiable and yet essential forces in models of the system. Systems' scenarios are not constrained by the language of quantities. They can be presented evocatively in powerful pictures and stories.

Deep listening and dialogue

If you go deeper into systems thinking, there are the disciplines of deep listening and dialogue. David Bohm says in *On Dialogue*[18] that the purpose of a deep dialogue is not to find a solution to anything. Indeed, he says, participants should enter into a dialogue without any common question in mind. Open-minded dialogue may lead each of them to internal questions, and perhaps the group may converge onto a shared question. However, the purpose of such a deep dialogue is to provide participants with a space to understand the world and themselves, which they are unable to when they seem to be always under pressure, in their professional and domestic lives, to manage and solve problems.

It is very difficult, amidst our lives' routines, to find the mental

---

[18] Routledge Classics, 2014.

and emotional spaces in which one can experience the Gita's wisdom: 'It is only the work and not the result that matters.' Or to find times and spaces in which one can merely observe one's thoughts without the instinctual urge to improve something or oneself. These are the times and spaces that practices of meditation are designed to create for us. Thus, deep dialogue, in Bohm's view, is a collective meditation to understand and learn, and not to achieve anything.

Aldous Huxley explains in *The Perennial Philosophy*[19] how the spiritual traditions within all religions—Hinduism, Christianity, Islam, Buddhism, Sikhism, Taoism and other faiths—are a search for 'the peace that passeth all understanding'. The search leads to insights about *what* and *who* 'I' am, and also to *why* 'I' am in the world. Insights into why I am here, i.e. the purpose of my existence, can lead on to an understanding of what is ethical conduct.

The four-step Learning-to-Learn Cycle

- Sensing/insighting
- Creating/visioning
- Prototyping/experimenting
- Reviewing/adjusting

Three disciplines to apply and develop in the Learning-to-Learn cycle

- Systems thinking
- Deep listening
- Ethics (of Citizenship)

---

[19] Harper Perennial Modern Classics, 2009.

PART D
Becoming a Leader

22

Learning to Lead

It is often noted that were India to attain the SDGs, the whole world would get much closer to attaining them, as India is a country of as many as 1.2 billion people. The only other country with over a billion people is China, which has progressed much further than India has in lifting its people out of poverty and providing them with basic education and public health facilities. China is now facing the poisonous side effects of its rapid economic growth for three decades on its environment and in the increasing inequalities when it comes to wealth.

Growth of India's GDP has been quite impressive recently, though it has not yet matched the relentlessly high GDP growth rates of China. Yet, India can claim that it is amongst the world's fastest-growing large economies. In fact, Indians can be proud that their country is the fastest-growing free market democracy in the world. However, India is also suffering from deterioration of its natural environment. It is also experiencing the pains of increasing inequalities of incomes and wealth, along with economic growth.

Indians are proud that their country is the world's largest democracy. But some worry that democracy has come in the way of India achieving the economic growth rates of China. They envy the Chinese authoritarian systems' capability to implement large-scale infrastructure projects and to get things done.

India has a lot of diversity. There are so many divisions within the country—political parties, regions, religions, economic strata, etc. The democratic process requires that different interests must be considered. However, the way the process is playing out in India is getting messier with the various groups acting blatantly in their self-interest. The parliamentary process, by which the many interests have to be finally reconciled, seems now to be anything but a good and reasonable process in India. Often, it is chaotic.

The acceleration of change in the country will require aligned action by many groups across the country—civic society, government, business and political parties. The problem for India's policymakers is that when they go one step forward, they invariably have to go half a step back because of protests from those who are adversely affected. Hence, the continuing concern amongst investors—can India carry on with its process of economic reforms swiftly?

There are many forums in India for discussion and debate amongst the many groups who must be consulted. These include the parliamentary process, as mentioned earlier. There are also many formal and informal meetings outside the parliamentary process, such as meetings sponsored by industry associations between business people and government, and in seminars sponsored by development agencies. Nevertheless, the alignment and action are insufficient. Hence, the frustration.

Many systemic and complex problems have to be solved to accelerate desired change in India to achieve the SDGs. Such problems require many people from different institutions, and with different perspectives, to work together. However, they are not working together effectively, which is why these problems have become endemic.

Realizing that India needed another, better approach for people to work together, to make growth faster, as well as more inclusive and more environmentally sustainable, many scores of Indians from many walks of life came together in 2000 to think about what this approach could be. They came together, in their personal capacities, as citizens who cared. They included senior government officials,

CEOs of large companies, economists, social scientists, teachers, social workers, women farmers, handloom weavers, students in college, and even homeless children living on the streets of Delhi.

They used the process of generative scenario thinking to put their perspectives together. This process has been used with good effect in many complicated situations. For example, it was used in early 1990s in South Africa, when the differences between the various races and political parties could have blown the country apart. Generative scenario thinking combines systems thinking with shared visioning to align aspirations, and to collectively analyze what must change in the system to achieve citizens' aspirations. I have described the process in my book, *Shaping the Future: Aspirational Leadership in India and Beyond*.[20]

Combining the diverse perspectives of many scores of people, a broad picture emerged of some principal forces shaping Indian society, its economy and politics at the turn of the millennium. Participants in the generative scenario thinking process had different views about how change can be brought about in such a diverse country with large aspirations yet to be fulfilled.

The perennial debate about whether an authoritarian system is necessary to suppress contentions and speed up implementation, and whether India would have been better off having less democracy until it was more economically developed, arose again. Opposing this view, others said that democracy should never be sacrificed just to impose order and to get things done. They cited the history of the Emergency imposed by Indira Gandhi, who had suspended civil liberties to impose more order. The trains had run more on time during the Emergency. But when Indira Gandhi called an election, expecting people's appreciation of the order imposed, she was soundly defeated.

The question of 'leadership' came up, as it always seems to, whenever there is need to bring about change in a complex system. 'Results will be produced if there are better leaders,' everyone

---

[20]John Wiley & Sons, 2002.

agreed. The participants were not satisfied with this answer. They went further to analyze what sort of leaders a large, diverse and democratic country must have to bring about more inclusive and more sustainable, faster growth.

Readers may recollect the 'three models' that a change-maker requires, explained in Chapter 13. They were: a model of what the system is; a model of how the system improves itself; and a model of how to help the system improve itself. Models of leaders who want to strengthen a system and make it better must be congruent with the model of what the system is and with the model of how the system improves itself. What sort of leaders are required to produce more inclusive and sustainable growth?

The scenario process generated four different models of leaders. Three of them conform to a top-down process of change; the fourth with a bottom-up process. In a top-down process, the leaders sit on top. In a bottom-up process, they are everywhere—at the bottom, in the middle, and some at the top too.

Four models of leaders

The four models of leaders and the models of change processes associated with them were described by the scenarists in four evocative pictures.

1. Buffaloes wallowing in a pond while the children wait

The first picture shows several large buffaloes wallowing in a pond on a hot summer day while a child is waiting patiently on the side of the pond. The buffaloes are persons in high positions and with important titles. They are in the government and in political parties. They include experts who advise them. The people expect these leaders to make change for the benefit of the people. When one buffalo gets an idea and wants to move, the others around it do not. So, the buffalo settles back. Then another gets an idea and wants to move, but the first prevents him, taking revenge for his non-cooperation in the first place.

While the buffaloes are wallowing around, unable to cooperate, the children are growing up. Even though the children are malnourished and not receiving good education, their blood, bones and brains are forming. They cannot wait for the leaders to make changes happen.

This is a model of top-down change, expected to be produced by people with authority advised by experts around them. This model of leadership at the top is the default model followed in large organizations, even in the private sector. It can work if there is a strong leader above them to make them cooperate with each other with the power to impose discipline on them.

Basically, this is the model that India had followed since its Independence, with a central government which retained most powers, and with centralized planning top-down. This model does not work well in an open, democratic, system, especially a complex one with a lot of diversity within, in which one-size cannot fit all.

2. Peacocks strutting while little birds are scrambling

This picture shows a resplendent peacock in the courtyard, in which grain has been strewn to feed the little birds. A few pigeons are pecking at the grain, avoiding the peacocks. Tiny sparrows are waiting on the side, hoping that the peacocks and pigeons will be satiated soon and will leave them some grain.

This is the model in which large-scale change in the economy and society is expected to be brought about a free market. The market is thrown up, and opportunities are given to people to make the most for themselves. The hope is that soon, somehow, the little people will have more too.

First, those who already have the wherewithal to take advantage of the opportunities—who already have some wealth, or access to people in power, or a better education than the rest—take advantage of the opening of the market. They become richer, more powerful, and their children get even better education at the world's best universities. Thus, the gap between those who have more and those who have less continues to increase.

The wealthy use their money to obtain support from others. They provide funds to political parties and take over media companies. People with more wealth than others become role models in capitalist societies. They have proven that they are smarter than others. They should be emulated. The media publish their opinions on almost everything. Their opinions are sought by people in government.

'Trickle down' is very slow. On the contrary, there is a 'trickle up' of power and wealth in this model. The rich become richer and more powerful.

3. Tigers growling and wolves prowling

In the middle of this picture a magnificent tiger is sitting in the forest. Some distance from him, amongst the trees, wolves are prowling. Little animals are cowering in the bushes.

This is the model of change brought about by instilling fear. Strongmen leaders and their bands of supporters intimidate the people. Opposition is eliminated, with violence if necessary. People lose their freedoms, but there is order. Things get done.

The scenarists found all three models of leaders and all three processes of change happening simultaneously in the country. Politicians and bureaucrats at the top continued to have power in the system. At the same time, wealthy and powerful people were becoming more visible. And, in interior parts of India, guerilla leaders and their followers, revolting against an unjust and incompetent government and against the exploitation of poor people by the wealthy, ruled large swathes of the country.

Overall, it was not a pretty picture. In every model, the leaders at the top stood above the rest, with their high positions, their wealth and their power to intimidate. In every picture, the people below continued to suffer. These models of change and leadership gave little hope for India's future.

4. Fireflies arising

Fortunately, as the scenarists widened and deepened their

exploration of the forces shaping India, they noticed a fourth model of change and of what leaders are.

In many parts of the country, they found people doing something, even if it was small, to improve the lives of people. They were not rich people, or politically powerful people, or people in positions of authority. They were ordinary people. What was extraordinary about them was their concern for the causes they were pursuing—the empowerment of women in villages, access to clean water, public health, education of children, etc.—and their determination to make a difference.

These leaders of change were tiny in comparison with the buffaloes, peacocks and tigers. However, they had an inner passion—an inner light, like fireflies have. They brightened up the lives of people, even if only a few. And they provided hope.

The picture the scenarists painted was of a dark, moonless night with many fireflies arising together. Each is tiny; each has its own light. When they rise together, they brighten up the night. They give hope that darkness can be turned to light.

Which is the appropriate model of leader to achieve the SDGs?

There can be many models of leaders. Each model must fit the context in which leadership has to be exercise—it must fit the model of the process of change appropriate for that context.

We have seen earlier that the model of change for solving systemic problems, such as those represented by the SDGs, must enable local, contextually appropriate solutions. It must also build local capacities to make improvements. A top-down, one-size-fits-all, model will not produce the outcomes desired. Therefore, capabilities to lead systemic change locally have to be widely dispersed at the bottom and in the middle of the system. Leaders at the top must be oriented towards building leadership and capacity for change throughout the system.

The scenarists concluded that large-scale outcomes cannot be produced by a few large-scale organizations with strong leaders atop them in a very diverse, large, complex and freedom-loving country like India. Large-scale outcomes will be produced by multiplying the numbers of fireflies throughout the system.

Since the scenarios were painted in 2000, with the four models of leaders embedded in them, I have seen the fireflies arising in India in thousands, perhaps millions. Thousands of young people are working with civil society organizations and not-for-profits. Many are donating their time to government organizations to make a difference to the lives of citizens less well off than them. Thousands of people, young and old, who have made it in businesses and large corporations, are taking time out to give back. Many people are forming alliances with each other to have greater impact.

Many are forming new forms of enterprises to enable more 'fireflies' to arise. They are creating learning spaces for fireflies to develop the orientations and skills they need to work as leaders and change-makers in an open system in which they are not the bosses but can be catalysts of large-scale change. Global Action on Poverty (GAP) brings hundreds of these fireflies together every year at the Sabarmati Ashram, where Mahatma Gandhi had lived and from where he had led the Dandi March. Here they learn from each other, and also from great change leaders who are showing the way, like Elabhen Bhat of SEWA and Muhammad Yunus of Grameen. The Vision India Foundation, formed by a young team of volunteers, organizes curated 'learning journeys' into India's districts for young people who want to make a difference. It organizes classes in spaces borrowed from universities, where teachers in development economics, political science, and leaders in change-management, share ideas with the 'fireflies' to sharpen their skills.

These enterprises are networks of persons who contribute voluntarily to form and sustain movements of transformation. It is hard to measure, in conventional terms, the 'size' of these catalytic organizations and 'scale' of their impact. They are not pursuing numbers. They want to learn how to become catalytic leaders and change the ways in which the system works to make the world better for everyone.

What makes a leader?

Further examination of the four models provides an insight into the essence of leadership. People emerge as leaders, not because of their endowments—their wealth and their social positions—but by the actions they take. They may have a high position, or wealth, or power to intimidate others. But this is not enough to make them good leaders. On the other hand, fireflies, who do not have any wealth, power or designated positions of authority, can be good leaders making changes to improve the lives of people at the bottom of the pyramid.

A leader is someone who takes the first steps towards something he or she deeply cares about, and in ways that others would wish to follow. We have encountered this definition of leadership before. Ravi, the CEO, and Priya, the young social worker, were both inspired by it. One of the best examples of this definition of a leader is Mahatma Gandhi. He was the brightest firefly in India, and perhaps the whole world, in the last century. He gave hope to hundreds of millions of people. He emerged as their leader, without sitting atop any large organization with an official position, and even though he had no wealth to give incentives to people to follow him and had no ability to beat them into submission (nor any desire to do so!). Millions followed him because he cared for what they cared about, which was their freedom from political, economic and social oppression. He demonstrated the depth of his care by his willingness to take the first steps towards a shared aspiration, at great risk to his own freedom and sometimes to his life.

Fireflies take the first steps to something they deeply care about, and they take those steps in ways that the people around them wish to follow. The people support such leaders because they see them working for the cause of the people, not for gilding their own wealth and power.

How are leaders made?

There is a popular saying, 'Some people are born leaders, others become leaders, and few have leadership thrust upon them.'

Consider the implications of this. If a person must be born a leader, then there is nothing much that those who are not fortunate to have been born as a leader can do to become one. When leadership is thrust upon some people, it is the demand for them to step and become leaders. However, they have to learn how to become a leader. Many fail to learn, and so fail as leaders. Therefore, the most relevant part of this old saying is how a person learns to become a leader. In this aspect too, we can learn a lot from Mahatma Gandhi. The title of his autobiography is *The Story of My Experiments with Truth* and he was a lifelong learner. Great leaders are always lifelong learners.

In summary, the three abilities leaders must have to make the world better for everyone are:

1. Self-starting ability

The first capability is a bias for action. Leaders are those who take the first steps. They find the path, and with their steps, make a path for others who follow.

Mahatma Gandhi was a man of action. He led from the front. The iconic statue, on Delhi's Mother Teresa Crescent, of Gandhi leading the march to the beaches of Dandi to harvest salt, depicts an old man, stick in hand, purposefully stepping forward, with a line of people following him. When India finally got its independence from the British, and the Indian tricolour flag was proudly hoisted in Delhi, Gandhi, who had led the freedom struggle, was not there to celebrate it. He was in Calcutta to stop the mayhem amongst Muslims and Hindus that had broken out with the Partition of India.

2. Submarine ability

Action is necessary. But it is the purpose of the action that will determine whether it is an ethical action.

A picture of an iceberg with most of its mass beneath the waterline, has been presented to the reader earlier. It explained that actions and events that appear above the waterline are guided by beliefs deep within the mind. Great leaders have the capability to look inside themselves, to examine their own motives for action and their own prejudices too. They have the submarine-like capability to go beneath the waterline within their own minds.

Gandhi was a great note-keeper. He listened to his mind, and recorded his reflections, questions and insights. One of his last notes, written in 1948, shortly before he was assassinated in a prayer meeting in Delhi, was advice to anyone confronted with doubt about whether the actions they intend are good actions. He wrote:

'I will give you a talisman. Whenever you are in doubt, or when the self becomes too much with you, apply the following test. Recall the face of the poorest and the weakest man [woman] whom you may have seen, and ask yourself, if the step you contemplate is going to be of any use to him [her]. Will he [she] gain anything by it? Will it restore him [her] to a control over his [her] own life and destiny? In other words, will it lead to swaraj [freedom] for the hungry and spiritually starving millions? Then you will find your doubts and your self melt away.'[21]

3. Helicopter ability

'Just do it', along with a swoosh, is the slogan used for advertising one of the world's largest brands of sports shoes. The slogan urges action. Leaders must act, as we have noted. But they must reflect too, on their motives for action, as well as what the consequences of their actions would be on the world around them.

Good leaders are systems thinkers. They are able to lift themselves up in a mental helicopter. They are able to observe patterns of forces in the world around them. They are able to see 'the system' of which they are a part. Systems thinking enables them to see obstacles as well as paths in the forest. With an

---

[21]Mahatma Gandhi, Last Phase, p. 65, Vol. II, 1958.

understanding of what the consequences of their actions could be, they can avoid unintended consequences from 'fixes that will backfire', which an urge to 'just do it' could cause.

All leaders, big or small, must be self-starters. They must also develop their submarine capabilities to strengthen their ethical orientation by conducting their own experiments with truth.

---

1. A leader is she or he who takes the first steps towards what she or he deeply cares about and in ways that others will wish to follow.
2. Three capabilities of good leaders:
   - Self-starting ability
   - Submarine ability
   - Helicopter ability
3. Good leaders are lifelong learners.

Index

(AI) deep learning systems 66
(AI) scientists 37
Academy of Management 113
Action-oriented managers 24
Affirmative action 38
AI 31,
regulating social media 36-37, 57
AI algorithm 48
AI laboratory 29, 31
AI machines 37
AI programmes 31, 37-38
appreciative inquiry, principles of 114
Aspen Institute seminar 161-162
global capitalism, challenges of 161
Aspire forum 92, 94, 141
group's collective learning 95
meetings 94-95
Aspire Foundation 138
attention deficit disorder 64, 172
authoritarian system 204

big data analysis' 56
big data analytics 31
and AI programmes 31-32
benefits of 31
broader social responsibility 114
business and ethics 114-15
business conversations 27
business management 17

business management schools, case study method 163
business world, learning to learn 188-189

Cacophony 173
capitalist economies 178
capitalist enterprises 178
centralized top-down programmes 176
CEO 6, 12-13
change-maker's own learning 27
chaordic system 87-90

chaotic systems 101
China, economic growth rates of 202
Chinese authoritarian systems 202
circular economy 132-35, 133f
civil society organizations (CSOs) 44, 138
Club of Rome's report 148-149
Tragedy of the Commons' 177
commercial client work 136
Communication 72
counter-arguments and counter-facts 72
good listening 72
practising good listening 73
speaking and listening 72

community outreach programmes 20
companies' CSR activities 7
Complex "self-adaptive" systems
  101-109
 adequate redundancy 108, 109
 aligned aspiration 104-5
 architectural principles of 102-104f
 economy of rules 108
 minimal critical rules 107-8
 permeable boundaries 105-7
Complex development challenges 180
Conservative families 53-54
Conservative views 67
Conservatives and liberals,
  competition between 71
Consultants 129, 13-32
conventional organizational form 179
corporate boards, failure of 6-7
Corporate citizenship 164-166
Corporate CSR 176-177
corporate frauds 6
corporate governance, breakdowns
  in 7
corporate investments 176
corporate managers', capabilities to
  manage risks 178
corporate social responsibility (CSR)
  7, 114
Crony capitalism 119
Cross model' conversations 20
CSR programmes 11
cultural psychology 49
cutting-edge technology challenges 29

day zero 4
debate 173
 purpose of 173-174
Debaters 174
Deep listeners 173
Deep listening and dialogue 198-199

collective meditation to understand
  and learn 199
Deliberation 174
democratic governance 178
Design thinking 141, 191-197
 After Action Reviews' 196-197
 creating/visioning 194-195
 prototyping/experimenting 195-196
 range scenarios 196
 reviewing/adjusting 196-197
 sensing/insighting 193-194
development circles, imperative to
  'scale up' 179
development management 140
digitized information 59
discipline within the organization 160
double-loop learning 22, 24
Dow Jones, meeting agendas 113-24
 business corporations, declining
  trust in 113
 establishing the 'business case' 114-
  15
 populism, causes for rise of 119
 socially responsible jobs,
  requirement for 116
 systems change 118

economic circular economy 134
Economics, science of 51
economies of scale 179-180
economists 17, 51-52
 computations 85
 internalizing forces 86
emotional intelligence 51
energy of commitment 24
espoused theory 22
ethical business enterprises, new
  forms of 166-68
 noble eightfold path 168
Ethical choices 164

Ethical decisions 164
Ethical foundations, origin of 48-56
Ethical orientation 158, 163-164
ethical principles
  distinction between 158
  evolve within communities and societies 159
Ethical problems 164
ethically correct action 158
European Enlightenment 100, 124, 181
  scientific approaches to learning 84

Fake news 35, 36
free agents 87

Game of Life 107-8
  evolving "life-like" patterns 108
generative scenario thinking 204
Global Action on Poverty (GAP) 209
global community trades 59
global network 89
global problem 90
global programmes 89
globalization agenda 59
golden rule of fairness 59
good business management 140
good democracies 67, 71-72
  sound lateral processes for deliberations 67
good listening 28
good management 132
  principles of 85
Great listeners 173

Hate speech 35
HR managers 21
human resource management 21-22
  professional processes of 22
professionalization of 21

IGSHG (inter-generational self-help group) 74, 88-89
  applying systems thinking more systematically to challenges 90
  turning development assistance on its head 89
India
  democratic process 203
  freedom movement 180-181
  future, Congress party's role in 181
  GDP, growth of 202
  parliamentary process 203
  policymakers, problem for 203
  political developments 60
  political movements in 60
  SDGs, systemic and complex problems 203
  WhatsApp, viral spreading of incitement 35
  wealth and income inequality in 129
Indian Administrative Service (IAS) 15, 16
Indian CSOs 138-39
Indian CSR law 135
Indian Foreign Service (IFS) 15, 16
Indian Institute of Management (IIM) 7-8
  career trajectories 8
Indian Institute of Technology (IIT) 7-8
Individualist moral codes 158
industrial design systems 198
IVI (Innovation- VUCA-Innovation) 186
IVI world 187
  sustainable competitive advantage 187

Japanese industrial organizations 188

Leaders 11-12
   different models of 204-209
   helicopter ability 212-213
   in organizations, skills of public speaking 170
   self-starting ability 211
   submarine ability 211-212
Leaders, different models of
   centralized planning top-down 206
   free market 206
   top-down change 205-206
   trickle down 207
Leadership 11
   ability 27
essence of 27, 210
   exercise of 26-27
   in a hierarchical organization 26
   in formal organizations 26
Leadership models 111-12
   complex self-adaptive system 111
   chaotic systems 111
   mechanical systems 111
learning agenda 83-84
Learning Cycle (PDCA) 188-189
   Adjust 189
   Check 189
   Do 189
   Plan 189
   steps of 189
liberal economists 120
liberal families 53-54
liberal ideologies, threat to 119
liberal views 67
limited liability corporation 164
linear thinking and systems thinking, conflict between 26
listening 169
   difficult to, reasons for 170-171
   to other viewpoints 169
   without preconceived notion 169

Listening deeply 172-173
   levels of depth 173
   preconceived notions 170
   to another 170

Machine values 67
management discipline 21
material circular economy 134
Millennium Development Goals 113
Minimal Critical Rules 108
Moral codes 52-53
   excessively individualist 53
   Individualistic (or egocentric) 52
   liberal ideas 53
   'Me' values 52-53
   morality, foundations of 52
   nature of 50
   of societies 52
   socio-centric 52
   socio-centric values 53

Nature, learning to learn 190-191
   self-adaptive' system 190
   sense and respond' 190
   sense, respond, observe and then adjust the response (SROA) 191
neo-liberal globalization 58
network of volunteers 182
networked organization 86-87, 176-185
   collective purpose 183
   framework for the structures of 184
   governance of the network 184-185
   shaping of 83-84
new technologies, developments of 35

objectionable speech 36
objective appraisal systems 21
older persons' associations (OPA) 89
OpenAI 30
Open-minded dialogue 198

Organization, networked form of 83
organizational functions 21
organizational learning 22
organizations' goals 24

PDCA Learning Cycle 189, 191
Philanthropy and corporate social responsibility (CSR) 135
plan for collaboration 23
plan for one's own learning 23-24
plan for systematic collaboration 23
plan of action 23
platform 183-185
Poor listening 28
problem-driven iterative action (PDIA) 190
pro-common man programmes 120
professionally managed institutions, pervasive growth of 159
public discourse, quality of 71
Pune Community Welfare Sanstha 19-20, 91

quarterly call with analysts 6

Rashtriya Swamsevak Sangh (RSS) 61
rational decisions 51
rational intelligence 51
rational management 17-18
reason and emotions 51-52
reorienting minds 174-175

Scenario thinking 196
school of development management 140
   conceptual theory of change 142, 143f-144f
   curriculum of learning, design of 144-145
   curriculum, designing of 141-142
   design-thinking consultant 141
   design-thinking services 141
   different paradigms 142-144
   systems thinking 141
   systems thinking lesson 142
   systems' approach to change 142, 143f-144f
self-justificatory economic theory 131
self-reliant organizations 42
self-righteous indignation 68
seventeen SDGs 44-45
Shallow listening 173
Silicon Valley Community Foundation 78-79
   drive to scale up 78
   'go-go' culture of 93
   technology 29
Single-loop learning 22
social change 26
social enterprises 139
social entrepreneur 92
   searching for better models of development 94
social harmony 159-160
social intelligence 51
social media 61-63
   and AI 36
   companies 32
   enterprise 160
   India, market for US social media giants 61-62
   misuse in India 62
   platforms 32, 183
   platforms, technologies applied 56
   promoters of 162
social sector
management of change in 138
   organizations 25
   scaling up' results in 25-26
   types 28

220 • *Transforming Systems*

society-centric moral code 159
socio-centric moral codes 54, 158
socio-economic development, trying to 'manage' 85
stakeholders 44, 45, 193, 194-195
  disagreements amongst 176
  need for effective partnerships 176-177
  problems with the approach 177
Sustainable Development Goals (SDGs)
  breaking complex problems into parts 45
  citizens' unmet needs 41
  competition 45
  demand for 'scaling up 179
  faster progress towards 178
  international charities 40
  making a city more livable for its citizens, formulating a plan 45-46
  NGOs', foreign sources of funds 41
  partnerships for 39-47
  partnerships working on shared goals 44
  professional management 45
  proposed urban mobility plan 46
  systems challenges 85
  systemic problems 176
  theories-in-use' 47
  training programme 45
  willing partners, international network of 40
System, purpose of 160
systemic actions 23
systems of compensation 21
systems orientation 85
Systems thinkers 193
Systems thinking 25, 75-77, 85, 146-149
  actions within silos 25
  cause-and-effect relationships 150
  essence of 79
  interconnections amongst views 152
  interdependence of forces 156
  into public discourse 148-49
  managerial instinct 25
  mapping in a systems diagram 153
  methods 86
  systemic' ability 150
  systems' level abilities 147
  theory-in-use 25
Systems thinking and deep listening (and dialogue) 197-198
  and 'shape' scenarios 198
  citizen-and-society systems 198
intangible values 198
  market' of exchanges—of give-and-take 198
Systems, models of 97-112
  Aligned aspiration 105-6
  Architectural principles 102-4
  development experts 100
  law of evolution 99
  leadership, modes 111-12
  scientific man's relationship with Nature 100
Systems, shape and structures of 79-82
  balancing loops' within systems 81
  complex socio-economic systems 79
  control on the population 79-80
  populations, changing shapes of 79
Systems, sizes and shapes of 77-79
  inequality increase within an economy 77
  larger size economies 77-78
  NGOs, drive to "scale up" 78
Systems, types of 101-102

Systems' structures 113-24
  deep-seated beliefs and ideologies 122
  knowledge of systems 124
  persistent and increasing inequalities 122-23
  Piketty's thesis 123
  prevalent 'scientific' way 123-24
  unlearning and relearning 121-24

Target groups for assistance 89
Technology 36
  promoters of 36
technology companies, ethics of 57
Technology, ethics of 63-66
  attention deficit disorder 64
  big data along with AI analysis 63-64
  conceptually gated communities 64
  ethical orientation 65-66
Facebook, access to 63
  internet and social media 64
  markets of one" 63
  social media, pernicious effects of 65

TED talks 170
theory-in-use 22
thought-provoking meeting 11
thoughts, bundle of 59-60
top-down planning systems 101
top-level private sector salaries 16
Total Quality Movement 188
Tragedy of the Commons 177-178
true leadership 11

UN Global Compact 113
unbridled technology 36
Universal Resource Identifiers (URIs) 107

Vision India Foundation 209
voluntary organizations 182
VUCA 186
  and innovation 186

World Economic Forum 139

yellow vests" movement 59